Personal Transformation From Within: The Power of Self Hypnosis For Lasting Change

Tim Moore

Published by Tim Moore, 2024.

While every precaution has been taken in the preparation of this book, the publisher assumes no responsibility for errors or omissions, or for damages resulting from the use of the information contained herein.

PERSONAL TRANSFORMATION FROM WITHIN: THE POWER OF SELF HYPNOSIS FOR LASTING CHANGE

First edition. July 1, 2024.

Copyright © 2024 Tim Moore.

ISBN: 979-8227653017

Written by Tim Moore.

Table of Contents

From Within: The Power of Self-Hypnosis for Lasting Change.
By Tim Moore, MHt

Welcome to the World of Self-Hypnosis

Welcome! I'm thrilled you have chosen to learn about the incredible power of your mind, and how to better harness that power to create the best life possible. It's a privilege to have the opportunity to guide you on this journey into the powerful world of self-hypnosis and the subconscious mind. This book is designed to be your roadmap as you explore the incredible potential of your mind. We'll dive into what hypnosis is, debunk some myths, and discover how self-hypnosis can help with everything from managing stress to boosting your physical well-being. Ready? Let's get started!

Let me start by telling you a bit about myself and how I got into exploring the mind. It all started back in the late '90s when I stumbled upon Neuro-Linguistic Programming (NLP). I was blown away by how it could create such rapid and significant changes in the mind. I got hooked thanks to people like Tony Robbins and NLP pioneers Richard Bandler and John Grinder. I wanted to know everything I could about this amazing tool and how the way we communicate with ourselves and others shapes our experiences, beliefs, and reality.

As a child, I was an extreme introvert. I had a lot of issues with feeling confident enough to engage with others and express myself. On the rare occasions that I tried to push myself, or fake it, I often felt extreme embarrassment afterward. I felt safe in my little bubble of isolation, but it held me back in just about every area of life, even as a child. Even though I knew my self-doubt wasn't rational, it was deeply ingrained in my subconscious.

My first experience with hypnosis was in elementary school when my mom took me to a local hypnotist to help with my grades, and while there was improvement, the hypnotist really didn't address the real root cause, which was all of the limiting beliefs that I had taken on as part of my identity. Until these beliefs changed, there wouldn't be permanent change to the reality I had created. *(This is a good reminder that as you work your way through this book, take a good hard look at the issues you want to work on and make sure that it's the real root cause. If you work on the surface issue, but not the root of the issue, you may not get the transformation you are looking for.)*

After barely graduating high school, with no clear life direction, I joined the military thinking it would help to break free from my self-imposed limitations. My desire to stay unnoticed worked well in boot camp (the longer you can go without the drill instructor knowing your name the better!).

After the military, I was certainly more confident, but still had this deep, heavy baggage I was carrying around, but I was trying hard to bury and hide it from the world around me.

I became a Police Officer in the small Chicago suburb that I grew up in, and even as a police officer, I still struggled with these underlying limiting beliefs. It wasn't until I discovered, and started using, NLP techniques as a detective that things really began to change. By building rapport and using NLP, I turned interrogations into casual conversations, getting quicker, more truthful confessions, and I found a new sense of confidence within myself. I found ways to work through the limiting beliefs I had taken on. I began to change my "I am" statement to one that I wanted. Most importantly I was able to see that the reality I had created was only my reality, and I could change it.

In 1999, I decided to leave police work because of the constant exposure to society's worst, as well as the politics that exist within a lot of small police departments. I knew that there were more opportunities and experiences for me waiting out there. Armed with this new NLP knowledge, I knew I could tackle new opportunities with confidence, I knew that I could create the reality I wanted for myself. I dove as deep as I could into understanding the mind, and how I could use these powers to improve my life. Early on in this new journey, I read a book that made one of the biggest impacts on my life. Looking back, this book, which nearly 3 decades later I still re-read, created the biggest change within me. The book was written by Dr. Joseph Murphy, "The Power of Your Subconscious Mind." This book was the door that led to my journey into the subconscious, self-hypnosis, and hypnotherapy.

Over the years I applied what I learned, created new businesses from the ground up, and had incredible life successes. I also had some pretty epic failures that earlier in life would have brought me to my knees and made me quit. During those failures, I applied my knowledge of the mind, and because of that, I was able to see them as nothing more than feedback. I could see them as an experience that I needed to have, needed to learn from, and ultimately used to bounce back even stronger.

Now, as I write this in 2024, I'm a Master Hypnotherapist, Clinical Hypnotherapist, Trainer of Hypnotherapy, NLP Practitioner, Empowerment and Success Coach, Author, and Speaker. All of the things a former extreme introvert should not be able to be. I'm still to this day always looking to learn more, improve, and create even more dramatic transformations for my clients, as well as for myself. It's been a wild ride, but I'm excited about what's next.

As a hypnotherapist, the transformations that I've seen sometimes defy logic. I've seen people who have had years-long, debilitating fears break free from those in single sessions. I've seen people who looked like they were at the end of their rope and hopeless when they first came to my office, completely transformed in only a few sessions. I've had clients who have dealt with past traumas their entire lives completely disconnect the negative emotions in under ½ hour. I've been part of complete turnarounds for clients dealing with anxiety, depression, chronic stress, and imposter syndrome, and I've seen chronic pain completely melt away. I have clients going through cancer treatments that experience little to no side effects and have even had clients go from stage 4 cancer to remission using the power of their minds. These are just a small sampling of the things that seem like miracles but are really just redirecting, and reprogramming their minds. They are learning to use powers they had all along, but that they weren't using.

I've also had some times where I wasn't able to help a client make a change. Despite having over a 90% success rate in making improvements with my clients, there are times and reasons when hypnosis won't help. There are, in my opinion, a few main reasons why. The first reason is that it was a change that they really didn't want for themselves, or the second reason is that there is a secondary benefit for holding on to the issue.

Let's look at the first one. You can't make change because someone else wants you to change, it has to be for you, and you have to really want and commit to it. If you want to stop smoking, but the reason behind that desire is that your doctor, spouse, kids, or anyone else is nagging or pressuring you, hypnosis likely won't create that change, or not to the degree it could. Our mind's job is to lead us towards pleasure and away from pain. If it knows that you are doing it for some other reason than your own desire, it will constantly lead you back to the habit that it knows deep down you don't want to break free from. It sees that as leading you towards what you really want.

Secondary benefits can also be a block to change. I had one client who came to me for pain, and while he didn't want to be in pain, his true reason for seeing me was as a temporary solution until his doctor would prescribe more narcotic pain medication. What he really wanted was the narcotic. Looking at that example, there is no way he would use his mind to release the pain because that would mean not getting what he really wanted, the narcotic. Because of that, his mind made sure that he held onto the pain, or he wouldn't get what he really wanted. People can also hold onto depression because of the secondary benefit of getting more attention, compassion, or a sense of love from others. They worry that taking away the depression (even though they don't want to be depressed) could take away the extra attention.

So make sure to ask yourself, is there any secondary benefit for holding on to my _________________ issue, and am I doing it because someone else wants me to change? If the answer to both is NO, you are an excellent candidate to see positive changes from hypnosis, whether self-hypnosis or working with a hypnotist/hypnotherapist.

To find out more about my services and a more in-depth look at the modalities I use, visit www.mindoverthebody.com[1]

Now Let's Get Started!

---

1.   http://www.mindoverthebody.com

change is possible.

Chapter 1: What is Hypnosis?

Welcome to the first chapter of the journey into the mind! Before we dive into the mechanics of self-hypnosis, it's important to understand what hypnosis actually is. Hypnosis might seem like a mysterious, scary, or magical process, but in reality, it's a natural state of focused attention and increased suggestibility.

Hypnosis is a state of mind that is simply a state of deep relaxation, focused attention, and an increased ability to respond to suggestions. When you're hypnotized, your brain enters a unique state of consciousness. Science has found that during hypnosis, certain areas of the brain become more active, while others become less so. This altered state allows you to bypass your critical thinking, and conscious mind and access your subconscious mind more directly. It's in the subconscious where all change ultimately needs to happen for it to be permanent.

Imagine your mind as an iceberg. The tip above the water represents your conscious mind—your active thoughts, goals, and awareness. The massive structure below the surface is your subconscious mind, where your beliefs, values, memories, habits, all sensory input processing, and automatic responses reside. It's in your subconscious where all of your bodily functions are controlled and regulated, Hypnosis helps you access this hidden part of the iceberg, allowing you to make meaningful changes at a deeper level. Now right where the water level is on the iceberg would be the critical factor (or critical faculty as some people refer to it) The critical factor is like the gatekeeper. It decides what gets into our subconscious, or what is rejected. In young children the critical factor doesn't exist yet, that's one reason hypnosis is really effective with small children, there is no wall between the conscious and subconscious. They can go into trance quickly (let's face it, they are always in a little bit of a trance state, to begin with) The young, developing mind is like a sponge, everything is easily accepted into the subconscious. It's also the reason we need to be careful in the information we give to kids. We often pass along our insecurities, biases, habits, limiting beliefs, and fears to our kids unintentionally. They are sucking up all of this information and it becomes the basis of their beliefs and identity. Sometimes, despite our best intentions, we give our kids a faulty map to work with, and as a result, they can have a harder time getting to their desired destination later in life because of our unintentional subconscious programming.

As teens and adults the critical factor is firmly in place and getting stronger all the time. For new information to get into, and be accepted by our subconscious we have to get past that gatekeeper if we intend to make deeper changes. That's exactly what hypnosis does, it creates an opening for us to slip past and give those positive suggestions where the conscious mind is less likely to disagree.

In this book, you will learn how to effectively, and quickly, induce the initial hypnotic state in self-hypnosis. It's during this initial state, or induction, that we get past the critical factor and can slip easily into the deeper parts of our minds where we can make amazing changes that can alter how the mind interprets new information.

Hypnosis is about directing the mind to the desired outcome, not manipulating it or tricking it. Your subconscious works nothing like your conscious mind. Here are a few unique qualities of the subconscious;

It can't process negative statements.

Because of this, we have to be careful to direct our minds to what we want, not what we don't want. If you say "I don't want to feel like a failure" you will certainly get more feelings of failure, but if you say, "I intend on being more successful", the mind hears that very differently and will help guide you to that success.

The subconscious doesn't know what's real vs. what's imagined.

When you picture something in your mind with lots of detail and feeling, your subconscious takes it as the real deal. This is why dreams can feel super realistic and why athletes and performers use visualization to up their game. When you imagine something vividly, your subconscious reacts as if it's actually happening, affecting your thoughts, actions, and even your body's responses.

The subconscious has no concept of time.

The subconscious mind operates in a timeless state. It doesn't differentiate between past, present, or future. Everything you experience or imagine is treated as happening right now. This is why past memories can feel so immediate and why future goals, when visualized, can seem so attainable or unattainable depending on past experiences. Your subconscious mind processes these experiences as if they are all part of the present moment. Using this timelessness is a powerful aspect of self-hypnosis because it means you can reframe past events, influence your current state, and set the stage for future success all at once. By harnessing this quality, you can make amazing changes in how you think and feel, regardless of when the original experiences occurred.

The subconscious is highly moral.

The subconscious mind is like a moral compass. It's deeply rooted in your values and beliefs, often steering you towards what you consider right and away from what you see as wrong (whether your perception is correct or not). This sense of morality is why you might feel a gut instinct or feel strong emotions when faced with ethical decisions. It's always working to align your actions with your core principles, beliefs, and values, even if you're not consciously aware of it. In self-hypnosis, this moral aspect can be a powerful tool. By reinforcing positive values and ethical behavior, you can direct your subconscious to support your goals and maintain integrity in your actions.

Its job is to lead you away from pain and toward pleasure.

The subconscious mind is wired to guide you away from pain and towards pleasure. This basic survival mechanism is designed to protect you from harm and ensure your well-being. When you encounter something that causes discomfort or pain, your subconscious mind remembers it and tries to steer you clear of similar situations in the future. On the flip side, it encourages behaviors and experiences that bring you joy and satisfaction. This drive for pleasure and avoidance of pain is a fundamental aspect of how your subconscious operates. In self-hypnosis, you can tap into this natural tendency by associating positive changes with pleasurable outcomes, making it easier to adopt new habits and behaviors that enhance your life.

The subconscious communicates differently.

The subconscious mind primarily communicates through images and emotions rather than words. While your conscious mind operates logically and verbally, your subconscious uses vivid, often symbolic imagery and direct emotional feedback to express deeper thoughts and desires. This visual and emotional language makes techniques like self-hypnosis and visualization so effective, as they align with how the subconscious naturally operates. By engaging with these images and emotions, you can tap into your own inner world to make lasting changes.

The subconscious automates habits and behaviors.

Once you learn something through repetition, such as driving a car or brushing your teeth, your subconscious takes over, allowing you to perform these tasks without thinking. This automation frees up your conscious mind to focus on new or more complex activities. The process of habit formation is deeply rooted in the subconscious, which is why changing habits can be challenging—it requires reprogramming this automatic system. In self-hypnosis, you can tap into this by creating new, positive habits and behaviors, making them automatic responses over time.

It stores all of your memories and linked emotions.

The subconscious mind acts as a giant storage system for all your memories and emotions. Even if you don't consciously remember every detail of an event, your subconscious holds onto these experiences, influencing your behavior and feelings. This includes everything from childhood memories to recent experiences, along with the emotions associated with them, good or bad. Because these stored memories and emotions can affect your reactions and decisions, accessing and understanding them through techniques like self-hypnosis can help you address unresolved issues and promote emotional healing. By working with your subconscious, you can bring these hidden influences to light and make positive changes in your life.

It controls all of your body functions.

The subconscious mind plays a crucial role in controlling your body's vital functions, including the regulation of the sympathetic and parasympathetic nervous systems. These systems are part of the autonomic nervous system, which operates without conscious effort to manage essential bodily functions. The sympathetic nervous system prepares your body for action, often referred to as the "fight or flight" response, by increasing heart rate, dilating airways, and releasing adrenaline. Conversely, the parasympathetic nervous system promotes relaxation and recovery, often called the "rest and digest" response, by slowing the heart rate, enhancing digestion, and conserving energy. Living with stress, anxiety, depression or any other negative emotional state can keep the sympathetic nervous system activated which can lead to not only negative mental issues but physical disease.

It works on the expectation of the outcome.

The subconscious mind operates largely on the expectation of outcomes. It anticipates results based on past experiences, beliefs, and the information it has stored. This means that if you expect something to turn out well, your subconscious mind aligns your thoughts, behaviors, and even physical responses to help achieve that positive outcome. Conversely, if you expect failure or negativity, your subconscious can inadvertently steer you toward those results. This expectation-based operation is why visualization and positive suggestions are so powerful; by vividly imagining and expecting positive outcomes, you program your subconscious to work towards making them a reality. In self-hypnosis, you harness this principle by reinforcing positive expectations, helping to align your subconscious efforts with your conscious goals and aspirations.

It's important to know how the subconscious mind works because without that understanding we can't communicate with it in the most effective way. By understanding the inner workings of the mind we can use these traits to lead it in the direction we want it to go. It is your faithful servant, your Genie in the bottle, but if it isn't clear what you really want, it will manifest what it thinks you want based on your conscious thinking. That can often be the exact opposite of what we really desire the outcome to be.

We will dive deeper into some myths and misconceptions about hypnosis in the next chapter (and there are a lot of them) but just to clear a few things up, let's start looking at a few. Hypnosis is one of the most powerful ways to make change that there is, but it's also one of the most misunderstood. One of the biggest misconceptions is that it is some magical process that results in losing control, or someone taking control over your mind. This couldn't be further from the truth, whether seeing a professional hypnotist or using self-hypnosis. When you're hypnotized, you're not asleep or unconscious, in fact, if you are asleep hypnosis won't work. While hypnotized you're simply in a state of focused relaxation, fully aware of your surroundings and in control of your actions. You can bring yourself out of hypnosis at any time.

Another myth is that only certain people can be hypnotized. Everyone can enter a hypnotic state with the rare exception of someone who may have experienced a traumatic brain injury. The other exception is people who resist or simply don't want to be hypnotized. When someone says to me, "You can't hypnotize me", my response is that they are correct. I simply don't have the power (no one does) to hypnotize someone if they don't want to experience hypnosis, and the same applies to self-hypnosis. Anyone who wants to experience the power of hypnosis can in fact enter a hypnotic state with the right guidance, techniques, and mindset. It's a natural ability that we all possess. If you've ever been so absorbed in a book or a movie that you lost track of time, that's time distortion and a form of natural hypnosis!

Hypnosis and states of trance have a long history. Ancient cultures centuries ago, including the Egyptians and Greeks, used trance-like states for healing and religious rituals. The modern practice of hypnosis began in the 18th century with Franz Mesmer, a German physician. You may have heard the term, being "Mesmerized" by something, Franz Mesmer is where that term originates from. Mesmer believed in a mysterious force he called "animal magnetism" (you've probably heard that term as well) that flowed through everything and that could induce trance states. Although his theories on animal magnetism were later debunked, Mesmer's work laid the foundation for modern hypnosis.

In the 19th century, Scottish surgeon James Braid coined the term "hypnosis," deriving it from the Greek word "hypnos," meaning sleep. Braid recognized that hypnosis was not a form of sleep but a unique state of focused attention. Since then, hypnosis has evolved into a respected therapeutic tool used by Hypnotherapists, mental health professionals, doctors, and self-improvement enthusiasts worldwide. It's a therapy that in 1958 was, and continues to be, recognized by the American Medical Association as a legitimate form of treatment when conducted by a trained practitioner.

So, how does hypnosis actually work? When you enter a hypnotic or trance state, your brain waves shift from the active beta state to the more relaxed alpha and theta states. In most cases self-hypnosis will bring you into the alpha state, while working with a professional can bring you into the even deeper high theta state. This brain wave shift allows your subconscious mind to become more receptive to suggestions. You are simply relaxing your mind to the point that the conscious mind steps out of the way for a little while and stops critically analyzing information so that we can communicate more directly with the subconscious. During hypnosis, you can give positive suggestions to your subconscious, helping to rewire your thought patterns, and behaviors, and even create physical change within your body. Those suggestions are created by our intention and communicated to the subconscious by creating images and emotions. It's about using the fact that the subconscious can't tell the difference between what's real and what's imagined and engaging your imagination in a positive way.

For example, if you want to quit smoking, you can use hypnosis to embed the suggestions and visualizations that you are a non-smoker. Over time, this suggestion can help change your habits and eliminate your cravings.

If you are experiencing pain or discomfort, you can use hypnosis to dissociate the pain from your body and experience complete comfort. Pain, while experienced in the body, is actually completely constructed by the mind as a way to bring our attention to something. It's the mind's warning signal as well as a way to keep us from overusing an injured area. Pain can be disconnected by the mind just as easily.

Hypnosis can also enhance your natural abilities. Athletes, musicians, and performers often use hypnosis to improve focus, reduce anxiety, and boost their confidence. By accessing the power of your subconscious mind, you can unlock your full potential.

You might be surprised to learn that you experience natural hypnotic states every day. Have you ever driven somewhere and realized you don't remember the last 3 exits you passed? That's called "highway hypnosis." Your conscious mind was focused on other things while your subconscious took over the driving almost as if you were on autopilot.

Meditation and mindfulness practices also induce a state similar to hypnosis, but while they share some similarities, there are also key differences. Self-hypnosis builds on these practices and makes it more powerful. Hypnosis is a structured way to achieve your goals and improve your life in more ways than you probably realize right at this moment.

When it comes to our physical and mental health it seems that it's all about the latest and greatest pill, (and generally, that pill comes with a long list of side effects) to overcome whatever issue we have. If there is a pill without a condition to treat, you can be pretty sure that a new illness, condition, or syndrome to use it on, even if trials show that that pill works no better than a placebo. If we, as a society, simply used our minds and the abilities it has readily available for us to use for changing the things we want to change, and to overcome what's affecting our life in a negative way, I believe the need for medical treatments and medications for things like pain, depression, anxiety, physical disease, among many other "Issues" would plummet.

Hypnosis is about making change. Those could be small behavior changes or big things like physical disease. The power to make that change is within you right now, and I am about to show you how to turn it on and transform your life.

Self Hypnosis vs. Professional Sessions

Let's take a look at self-hypnosis and how it differs from going to a certified hypnotist or hypnotherapist.

While the process and experience can be quite different, the reality is that all hypnosis is, at its core, self-hypnosis. The change comes from you creating those suggestions, images, and emotions in your mind in a trance state, and your subconscious accepting those suggestions, not someone else going into your mind and making that change.

So, if all hypnosis is ultimately self-hypnosis is it as effective and powerful as going to a trained professional? The answer is always, it depends. Self-hypnosis is like anything else, it takes practice and commitment. When a client comes to me for professional sessions I make clear that I don't have a magic wand. While I can, and usually do, help them get results quickly, we also have to manage expectations. Immediate results are possible and do happen, but in a lot of cases we also have to realize that if we have been dealing with an issue for a long time, it might take a little time to fully resolve those issues. The key is not to give up and to keep moving forward in the direction of the change you want. The same goes for self-hypnosis. It's a powerful tool and can create amazing changes. As you begin this new journey into your mind, you should have the expectation that you are making a change, but let's not expect to change a lifelong issue in your first attempt within 20 minutes. The key is repetition, practice, and commitment.

The depth of trance is usually different in self-hypnosis than in professionally conducted sessions. Even I, after all this time, can't go as deep into a trance with self-hypnosis as I can when hypnotized by someone else. The good news is that for a lot of issues, you don't need a deep trance to make change, and the more you practice the deeper you will be able to take yourself.

Disengagement of the conscious mind can be harder in self-hypnosis as well. Because you are the one who will be giving yourself suggestions, you need more conscious engagement. That's where the repetition comes into play, the more you take yourself into the hypnotic state the more you can disengage that critical-thinking mind.

For deeper issues or change it can be a great thing to combine self-hypnosis with some professional sessions. This can sometimes be the quickest way to create the change you want.

Ultimately whatever you choose, self-hypnosis, or a combination approach, it's you who is going to create the change. That power is one you already have readily available to you, and it's just waiting to be activated.

In the next chapter, we'll tackle some of the other common myths and misconceptions about hypnosis. Understanding what hypnosis is and isn't will help you embrace its true potential. Get ready to dispel some myths and unlock the door to a more empowered you!

Chapter 2: Myths and Misconceptions

"Focus your eyes on my swinging pocket watch.....your eyes are getting heavy ..... now by the power of hypnosis, cluck like a chicken!!"
That's what a lot of people think I do when first hearing that I am a hypnotist. They think I must make people do silly things, or that it must be fake. While I'm not against using hypnosis for entertainment, and in fact have been known to do just that, I spend a lot of time breaking down that false assumption that hypnosis is primarily for entertainment. Hypnosis is something that is recognized as primarily a therapeutic modality, including by such organizations as the American Medical Association, that can <u>also</u> be used for entertainment, not the other way around.

The truth is however that a lot of people have only been exposed to hypnosis by seeing a video online, attending a comedy stage show, or watched a movie where someone completely takes control of someone else's mind. While those performances can be entertaining, they are very different from the incredible therapeutic, life changing power that truly exists through hypnosis.

So, can hypnosis make someone act silly? Yes, if they are willing and have an assumption that they are going to act silly. When you see a comedy hypnosis show, the participants are selected because of their high level of suggestibility uncovered during some suggestibility tests conducted prior to engaging those people in the main performance. They become a willing participant in stage hypnosis, not someone doing something against their will. There are fun and entertaining things that you can do with hypnosis, but making people do things against their will just isn't one of them. Putting the entertainment aspect or things you may have seen on the internet aside, hypnosis requires that the suggestion given to someone, or yourself, aligns with the person's goals, values, desires, and beliefs and that the suggestions given are structured to what they want, not what they don't want.

Let's take a deeper look at some of the myths and misconceptions about hypnosis.

MYTH: Hypnosis is a truth serum or it can make me remember things I've forgotten in the past.

The idea that hypnosis can unlock hidden or repressed memories is a controversial topic. While hypnosis can enhance memory recall, it can also create false memories. The mind is highly suggestible in a hypnotic state, and leading questions or suggestions can lead to the creation of memories that never actually occurred. This is one of the reasons that it is important to use language wisely when creating suggestions, including during self-hypnosis.

MYTH: You can get "Stuck" in Hypnosis

Nope, it is completely impossible to get "Stuck" in hypnosis. You are in control the whole time and will eventually just open your eyes and come out of hypnosis. That applies to both self-hypnosis and working with a professional hypnotist.

MYTH: Hypnosis only works with weak-minded people

It is often the exact opposite. Hypnosis requires concentration and focus, and people who are intelligent and capable of sustained attention are often more successful with hypnosis.

MYTH: Hypnosis is Dangerous:

Some people believe that hypnosis is a dangerous practice that can harm the mind, despite no evidence that anyone has ever been harmed through the use of hypnosis. Hypnosis is a natural state and 100% safe and side effect free.

MYTH: Hypnosis is Just Sleep:

Not only is hypnosis not sleep, it won't work should you fall asleep or listen to recordings while sleeping. You are awake, but in that relaxed alpha brain wave frequency state, completely aware of what's happening.

MYTH: People Can Be Hypnotized Against Their Will:

Hypnosis requires the consent and cooperation of the individual. You cannot be hypnotized unless you are willing and open to the process.

One word of caution before we continue, hypnosis itself is completely safe, however, If you're using hypnosis to explore traumatic or emotional past memories, it's best to work with a qualified professional who can guide you safely through the regression process. Oftentimes exploring the past can create an abreaction that a professional hypnotist or hypnotherapist can help navigate and disconnect the emotional response.

If you are dealing with a serious diagnosed medical or mental health issue, hypnosis can be used as a complementary practice alongside other forms of treatment and self-care. It should be one part of your overall wellness recipe.

We've addressed some of the most common myths and misconceptions about hypnosis. It's not mind control, you can't get stuck in a trance, and it's not the same as sleep. Hypnosis is a safe, natural practice that anyone can benefit from, regardless of their level of skepticism.

In the next chapter, we'll dive into the mechanics of self-hypnosis. You'll learn how to hypnotize yourself, step by step, and discover techniques to achieve deep relaxation and focused attention. Get ready to unlock the door to your subconscious mind and take control of your personal transformation!

Chapter 3: The Mechanics of Self-Hypnosis

Now that you have a solid understanding of what hypnosis is and have debunked some common myths, it's time to dive into the practical side of self-hypnosis. In this chapter, we'll explore the step-by-step process of hypnotizing yourself. With practice, you'll be able to enter a hypnotic state at will, unlocking the door to your subconscious mind.

The first step is simply finding somewhere where you can comfortably relax and not be disturbed. You want to be comfortable, but you also want to be able to stay awake during your self-hypnosis session. Remember, hypnosis requires a certain amount of conscious awareness. While we want the conscious mind out of our way, we still need it to understand, and work with our intended outcome. When I work with clients in person I can almost always get them in a very deep trance, and the possibility of them falling asleep is pretty high. It's for that reason that I intentionally have a chair in my office that isn't overly comfortable. Wherever you intend on using self hypnosis, your goal should be to stay awake through the session.

The next step is the induction, or initial stage of hypnosis. The induction is where we get past that critical factor and slip undetected into the subconscious. Inductions can take anywhere from 1 second to 15 or more minutes. I prefer quick inductions. Why waste time inducing the initial state of hypnosis when we can spend that time on our suggestions? Now at first you may need some additional time, but with practice you can learn to drop down into the initial state of hypnosis almost immediately.

I'll break down and explain several different inductions. Use what feels right for you.

Rapid Self-Hypnosis Induction

This is one of my favorites, and the one I use when doing self-hypnosis myself. With practice it is a technique that can almost immediately put you in that initial state of hypnosis.

To start, make yourself comfortable, I prefer sitting instead of laying down as there is less chance of falling asleep..

Close your eyes and take a breath in through your nose. Feel the cool, fresh air enter your nostrils. Exhale and feel the warm air leave your body.

Now inhale again, but this time hold your breath. When you can no longer hold that breath, exhale rapidly, say the word "Sleep" in your mind and allow your body to completely relax and collapse down. See all stress and tension leave your body and mind. When I say completely relax, I mean completely.

Now, as we discussed, you won't be asleep, but your mind and body know that as a trigger word for complete relaxation. Pretend that your body did go to sleep. Don't sit straight and rigid like the posture a lot of people use while meditating. Let your body slump down and fully relax. Your body and mind are always working together and creating physiology that mimics your body being asleep will take your mind along with it.

Now imagine a big wave of relaxation flowing down from the top of your head down to the tips of your toes. Try and feel it like a lateral wave of relaxation.

Finally do a body scan and if there are any areas of your body that you still feel stress or tension, imaging that wave washing it away.

Eye Focus Induction

Get comfortable in your "Hypno-Chair". Once you are comfortable, simply allow your eyes to roll back slightly so that you are looking up. Don't roll them back to the point of straining, just enough so they aren't looking straight ahead.

Now find a spot to focus on either on the wall or ceiling depending on where you are looking. Keep your focus on that spot. It's ok if you need to blink, just return your focus to that spot.

While keeping your focus there, notice your peripheral vision. Notice (while still looking at your spot) what's to your left and right, above you and below you.

Now begin relaxing all of the muscles that surround your eyes.

You will likely notice your eyes feeling heavier, tired, fluttering, watering, or going in and out of focus. Try to keep them open a little bit longer and just let your mind wander to wherever it wants to go.

When they get to a point where they really want to close and just relax, gently let them close and say the word "Sleep" in your mind (again, not really sleeping). Let your body slump down and fully relax.

See that wave of relaxation from your head to your toes, and scan the body for any stress or tension that remains.

Modified Elman Induction for Self-hypnosis

Dave Elman was one of the early modern pioneers of medical hypnosis. His simple but effective induction is still used today by a lot of hypnotists around the world. If you have worked with me in private sessions, you've likely experienced my version of this induction. Here I've adapted it for self-hypnosis.

Go ahead and make yourself nice and comfortable.

Simply close your eyes and allow your eyes to roll back slightly as if you are looking at a spot on the inside of your forehead.

Relax all the muscles that surround your eyes, and relax them to the point where they wouldn't open even if you wanted them to. You're in control and only you can do that. Now, once you're sure you have them relaxed to the point where they won't open, test them to make sure they won't open for a few seconds, then stop testing.

Now imagine that wave of relaxation flowing from the top of your head down to the tips of your toes, moving through every cell in your body, relaxing down deeper.

Now, say in your mind, on the count of 3 open your eyes momentarily (½ second is all you need) do that and then when your eyes open say the word "Sleep" in your mind, close your eyes again and let yourself go deeper relaxed. Do this 3-5 times allowing yourself to go deeper and deeper relaxed every time you close your eyes.

Now you are going to start counting backwards from 100, but you are going to relax your mind to the point that those numbers disappear and you just can't see the next number. It might take until you get to 98 or 97, but really see those numbers disappearing. Between each number say in your mind (or out loud) "Relaxing deeper". So it would be ... 100 ...Relaxing Deeper...99....Relaxing Deeper...98.... Remember, it's about allowing those numbers to disappear by relaxing your mind.

NOTE: This induction uses a technique called fractionation, opening your eyes brings you out of trance and closing them saying "Sleep" puts you back into trance. It's been shown that each time you go back into that trance you go deeper. In almost all of my inductions with clients I will use fractionation during the induction. Feel free to add this to any of the inductions in this book.

Body Scan Induction

This is a slower progressive induction, but it is very effective and a great one to use as you begin using self-hypnosis. For clients using self-hypnosis for pain or discomfort, you may want to use one of the more rapid inductions, but for everyday issues or changes this induction can be very effective, and relaxing.

Make yourself comfortable.

Starting with your toes, notice how they feel, pay attention to any sensations in them. Now tighten them and contract the muscles. Hold them tight for about 2 seconds, then release and relax them as much as you possibly can.

Say in your mind. "Relaxing Deeply"

Now move up to the calves, and notice any sensations in the calves. Now tighten, then release and relax..." Relaxing Deeply"

Move up to the knees, thighs, butt, stomach, chest, arms, hands, neck, and then your face.

Allow each body part to completely relax.

When you've done your whole body, scan it for any stress or tension that remains and if you find any areas that are still tight, let them relax even more.

Now you can go into a deepener, or add in fractionation by counting to 3, opening your eyes briefly, closing them while thinking "Sleep" and relaxing down deeper each time.

Visualization Induction

This one is all about using your imagination to take you into a state of deep relaxation. The key is to visualize as vividly as you can. This is a great induction for highly visual people.

Once again, get comfortable.

Close your eyes and take a few deep breaths, Notice the coolness of the air as it enters your nose, feel the warmth as it leaves.

Continue to just focus on your breathing.

Now imagine yourself being transported through time and space to a place where you can relax fully. A place of total peace and safety. This could be a tropical beach, a forest, next to a river. Wherever you want to go to relax, just go to that place and focus on all of the little details one by one.

Make it a vivid mind experience. I'll use a forest example to give you the idea of the detail you want to imagine.

Imagine yourself transported to a beautiful forest, the most beautiful forest you've ever seen.

Notice the lush green grass blowing gently in the warm breeze.

Feel the warmth of the sun shining down on your face.

Notice the deep blue color of the sky. See one soft white fluffy cloud floating by.

Notice the feeling of the ground under your feet.

In the distance imagine the sounds of birds singing their beautiful songs.

Now imagine a patch of wildflowers, with all of your favorite colors.

Hear the sound of a gentle flowing river in the distance as the water cascades over the rocks.

Notice now that you are standing on a path and imagine that you begin walking that path. As you make your way through the forest you find that you relax deeper and deeper..

Now, that's one example, if you are on a beach, feel the sand under your feet and hear the waves. Imagine walking up to the edge of the water and feeling the cool water as it touches your toes. Wherever you are, see it all like you are there experiencing it in the present moment.

Step 2 Deepeners

Now that you have induced the initial state of trance, we want to deepen the trance. We want to get down into that low alpha brain wave frequency.

The deepeners I use all involve counting down and with each number allowing the relaxation to go deeper.

The Staircase Deepener

After you have done the induction, imagine yourself standing at the top of a staircase with 10 steps leading down. This staircase has a nice sturdy handrail to hold onto. Imagine that with each number you count down, you become more and more relaxed. Say "Deeper" in your mind after each step down you take.

10.....Deeper....9.....Deeper.....8........Deeper...........

When you get to one, really allow yourself to relax as deeply as you can.

The Elevator Deepener

Very Similar to the staircase deepener, but with this one imaging yourself on the 10th floor of a building. See yourself getting into the elevator, the doors close and push the button for floor 1. Then do your countdown.

10.....Deeper....9.....Deeper.....8........Deeper...........

Melting Through the Floor

With this deepener imagine that the chair you're sitting on begins to slowly drift down through the floor and goes deeper with each number. Imagine your body getting heavier with each number.

10.....Deeper....9.....Deeper.....8........Deeper...........

Let's Recap

Now you have several inductions and deepeners that you can use to get into that hypnotic state. Pick the ones you like the best. Now it's time to start the suggestions for the specific issue you are working on. In the following chapters I have suggestions for you to use, or you can use my suggestions as a starting point to come up with your own, but remember, focus on the outcome you want, not what you don't want.

Practice Makes Perfect. Self-hypnosis is a skill, and like any skill, it gets better with practice. The more you practice, the easier it will become to enter a hypnotic state and achieve your goals. Don't be discouraged if it takes a few tries to get the hang of it. With persistence and patience, you'll become a skilled self-hypnotist.

Chapter 4: Crafting Suggestions, Anchoring, and Emerging

In the following chapters you will find sections on some of the most common issues or improvements that people often use self hypnosis for, however we are all individuals with very different experiences, needs, issues or areas of life that we want improvement in.

In my practice, I use my conversation with my client to craft the suggestions I use in the session, and because no 2 people are ever the same, no 2 sessions are ever the same either. The suggestions are the key ingredient in the recipe, so it's important to make sure they are the right ingredient.

Once you get really clear on the outcome you want, and get good at knowing the suggestions that align with that goal, you will find that you can come up with positive suggestions and visualizations quickly and easily.

There are a few guidelines that you want to follow when crafting suggestions or suggestions.

1. The outcome is stated as a positive, never a negative.
    a. Each day I am becoming healthier.
    b. I find that everyday I enjoy school more and more and I find that I enjoy learning.
    c. I am becoming more and more confident.
    d. I am no longer held back by past limitations, I'm growing stronger each day.
2. You make it believable for the mind. If you make it too far fetched your mind will simply reject the suggestion.
    a. Money is moving towards me vs. I'm already rich.

    b. I am learning to enjoy healthier food, and as a result, I am getting closer and closer to my weight goals vs. I'm fit and skinny.

    c. I perform at my best with confidence and ease. vs. I'm the champion

    d. My body is healing and becoming stronger every day vs. I'm fully healed

3. Visualize the transformation.

    a. For weight loss, see your new body in a mirror and step into it to try it out.

    b. For confidence, see yourself giving that presentation confidently and perfectly.

    c. For sports, see yourself performing at the top of your game.

    d. For health, see your body healing in the specific area that the healing needs to happen.

4. Repetition is key

    a. The mind loves repetition, repeat your outcome at least 3 times while visualizing the desired outcome.

5. Future pace

    a. See yourself in the future once this issue, problem, or improvement has been made. See yourself in that future moment knowing that you are no longer affected by it. Feel the emotion from that that you would feel (confident, happy, free, etc.) and bring those feelings back with you into the present moment.

Anchoring (optional)

When we are sad or upset, a hug can usually make us feel better. That hug is an anchor that was probably installed from birth, from the first time you cried and someone picked you up to comfort you. We can also use anchors to help us recall positive states while in hypnosis. These anchors can be helpful for times when we need to recall confidence, calmness, happiness, or just about any other positive emotion. An anchor can be a word, a touch to a specific area of the body, or even just putting your thumb and index finger together.

While you're in the state of hypnosis, create that image of having accomplished whatever it is you are working on. Make it real. See what you would see, hear what you would hear, and feel what you would feel. Make the image brighter, more vivid. Feel the emotions you would feel. Now activate your anchor while feeling it (word, touch, fingers together) release the anchor when the emotions begin to fade. Repeat it as often as possible to really link that word or movement to that feeling.

Emerging

So now you induced the initial state of hypnosis, Deepened the trance, gave suggestions, possibly anchored a positive emotion, and future paced. Now it's time to come back out of the hypnotic state. Rather than simply open your eyes, it's always a good idea to bring yourself out of the stance slower. The best way to do that is counting yourself up (rather than counting down like we do in the deepeners).

Simply tell yourself that the suggestions you gave yourself will get stronger by the day and now count from 1-5, and at the count of 5 you will open your eyes and feel wonderful.

"These suggestions I have given myself will get stronger by the day, because these are suggestions that I want. These suggestions will be accepted by my subconscious mind as the truth. Now I will count from 1-5. With each number I count I will become more aware and awake. When I reach number 5 I will open my eyes and I will feel wonderful, as if I've just emerged from a wonderful restful nap and ready to take on the day."

1. Body, mind, and spirit fully integrated.
2. Beginning to feel wonderful
3. Breathing deeper now
4. Becoming more aware of the sounds around me
5. Eyes open, feeling wonderful.

Good Job! Now let's get ready to stretch our mind muscles with a few experiments! In the next chapter, we'll put your self-hypnosis skills to the test with some fun and simple experiments. These exercises will help you build confidence in your abilities and see the power of self-hypnosis in action.

It's important to remember that like any skill, learning self hypnosis might take practice and persistence. It can be a part of your daily life. The more you engage your subconscious the easier it will become.

28

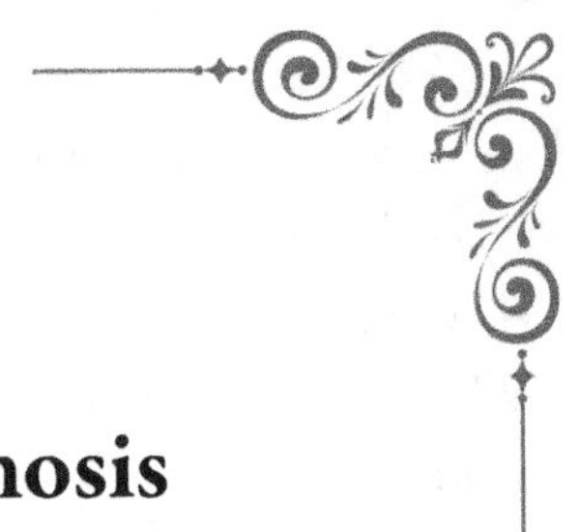

Chapter 5: Self-Hypnosis Experiments

Now that you've learned the techniques of self-hypnosis, it's time to put your skills to the test with some fun and simple experiments. These exercises will help you build confidence in your abilities and see the power of self-hypnosis in action.

Don't worry if you aren't successful with all of these the first time through. It's a new skill and one that takes practice and repetition. Keep going and you will see results.

Experiment 1: The Lemon Test

The lemon test is a classic hypnosis experiment that I often use as a warmup exercise when I do group hypnosis events. The lemon test helps demonstrate the power of visualization and suggestion. It's a great way to show you that the mind is fully in control of the body, not the other way around.

1. Begin by sitting in a comfortable position and closing your eyes.

2. Enter a state of relaxation using one of the induction and deepener techniques you've learned.

3. Once you're in a hypnotic state, either visualize the following on your own, or you can have someone slowly ready the script to you as you imagine the following:

Imagine that you're in your own kitchen right now. Picture it in your mind. The room is well-lit, and you can see your refrigerator standing there.

As you stand in your kitchen, you suddenly remember that you have a bright, yellow lemon in your refrigerator. It's sitting there, perfectly chilled. Take a moment to visualize the refrigerator and the lemon inside. See the lemon clearly in your mind's eye.

Now, imagine reaching out and opening the refrigerator door. Feel the cool air brush against your face as you do so. The fridge light comes on, and you can see the shelves filled with food. Focus on the crisp, inviting sight of that lemon.

Extend your hand and reach for the lemon. Feel its coldness as you touch it. Take a moment to hold it in your hand. Notice how real it feels in your imagination.

Bring the lemon up to your nose and take a deep breath. Can you smell the fresh citrus scent? It's tangy and refreshing, isn't it? Take another deep breath and let that lemony aroma fill your senses.

Now, imagine taking a knife and cutting a slice from the lemon. As you do this, notice the spray of lemon juice that bursts from the fruit. Imagine placing that lemon slice in your mouth and taking a bite. Feel the sensation as the tartness of the lemon juice hits your taste buds. It might make your mouth pucker a little.

As you continue to chew that lemon, notice that your mouth waters more. Pay attention to the way your body responds to this imaginary experience. Some people might notice a tingling or salivation sensation. Others might experience a heightened sense of taste.

Now, go ahead and gently place the imaginary lemon back into your refrigerator. Close the refrigerator door and take a deep breath. You can let go of the taste and sensation.

If you find that you have more saliva in your mouth than when you started or reacted to the imagined lemon in any way, you've successfully used self-hypnosis to create a vivid sensory experience. Your mind didn't know that there was no real lemon, it thought it was real and created the extra saliva.

Experiment 2: The Hand Levitation Test

The hand levitation test demonstrates the power of suggestion and the connection between your mind and body.

1. Sit in a comfortable position and close your eyes.

2. Enter a state of relaxation using your preferred induction and deepener technique.

3. Once you're in a hypnotic state, focus on your right hand.

4. Imagine a string attached to your right wrist attached to a giant helium balloon, gently pulling your hand upward.

5. Feel your hand becoming lighter and lighter as if it's being lifted by an invisible force and imagine that arm as hollow and weightless.

6. Allow your hand to rise slowly, feeling the sensation of it lifting on its own.

If your hand starts to lift, even slightly, you've successfully used self-hypnosis to influence your physical body.

Experiment 3: The Arm Rigidity Test

The arm rigidity test shows how powerful suggestions can be in creating physical sensations.

1. Sit comfortably and close your eyes.

2. Enter a state of relaxation using an induction and deepener technique.

3. Once in a hypnotic state, focus on your left arm.

4. Imagine your left arm becoming stiff and rigid as if it's made of solid steel.

5. Feel the stiffness spreading from your shoulder to your fingertips, making it impossible to bend your arm.

6. Try to bend your arm while maintaining the suggestion of rigidity.

If your arm feels stiff and difficult to bend, you've successfully used self-hypnosis to create a physical sensation.

Experiment 4: The Temperature Test

The temperature test demonstrates the power of suggestion in altering your perception of temperature.

1. Sit comfortably and close your eyes.

2. Enter a state of relaxation using an induction and deepener technique.

3. Once in a hypnotic state, focus on your right hand.

4. Imagine your right hand becoming very warm, as if it's being bathed in sunlight.

5. Feel the warmth spreading through your hand and fingers.

6. Now, imagine your left hand becoming very cold, as if it's submerged in icy water.

7. Feel the cold sensation spreading through your left hand and fingers.

If you notice a difference in temperature between your hands, you've successfully used self-hypnosis to alter your sensory perception.

Experiment 5: The Confidence Booster

This experiment uses self-hypnosis to boost your confidence and self-esteem.

1. Sit comfortably and close your eyes.

2. Enter a state of relaxation using an induction and deepener technique.

3. Once in a hypnotic state, visualize a situation where you want to feel more confident, such as giving a presentation or meeting new people.

4. Imagine yourself in this situation, feeling calm, confident, and in control.

5. Repeat positive suggestions to yourself, such as "I am confident," "I am capable," and "I can handle this."

6. Visualize the successful outcome of the situation, feeling proud and accomplished.

By repeatedly practicing this exercise, you can build your confidence and enhance your self-esteem in real-life situations.

Experiment 6: The Stress Reliever

Use this experiment to reduce stress and promote relaxation.

1. Sit comfortably and close your eyes.

2. Enter a state of relaxation using an induction and deepener technique.

3. Once in a hypnotic state, visualize a peaceful place, such as a beach, forest, or garden.

4. Imagine yourself in this place, feeling calm and relaxed.

5. Focus on the sights, sounds, and smells of your peaceful place, immersing yourself fully in the experience.

6. Repeat calming suggestions to yourself, such as "I am relaxed," "I am at peace," and "I am calm."

Practicing this exercise regularly can help you manage stress and maintain a sense of inner peace.

These experiments are a fun way to build your self-hypnosis skills and experience the power of your mind. Some of these may take practice, the more you use self hypnosis the easier it becomes to create these sensations.

Now it's time to start addressing the things that YOU want to improve, eliminate, or create. The chapters that follow are broken down by specific issues that are common for people to be dealing with in life.

You will find each technique will all share common elements:

- The induction
  - Creates the initial state of relaxation or trance
- The deepener
  - Deepens the trance state
  - Not used with prepubescent children

- The visualization and setting
  - Creates the initial scene for the mind
- Engaging the imagination
- Positive Suggestions to create the outcome we want
- Returning to reality
- Returning to awareness

Whether you are using one of my techniques, or creating suggestions of your own, it's important to use the structure of the techniques in that order.

It can also help if you have some soft, meditative, or Zen music playing in the background. It can help calm the mind and at the same time cover up some outside noises that might distract you.

Now let's make some positive changes. You can go to the index and find sections of the book that apply to the changes you want to make, or you can explore each section to see how these techniques can be beneficial for you, or someone you care about.

Chapter 6: Self-Hypnosis for Teens and Parents

Teenagers face unique challenges, and parents often struggle to help them navigate these formative years. In our entire lifetime, the teen years are when our minds undergo the most dramatic transformation in our lifetime. It's during these years that that critical factor begins coming into play. We all remember those years well. It's the time when we start becoming more independent, have our own thoughts and feelings about things, and often are sure we are right about everything and our parents are complete idiots.

This is the time when beliefs and values can get locked into the subconscious. It's a time when behaviors can change for better or worse, and a time when our friends, rather than our parents, can have a bigger influence on the development of our identity.

This is a time when these young men and women can feel a tremendous amount of social stress, grades can drop off from a lack of focus, their self-esteem can drop as other kids mature faster, or they may find themselves on the receiving end of bullying.

For parents it can also be a stressful, scary time as well when our children transition into young adults and they begin having a need for more independence, and for new levels of privacy.

This chapter offers specific techniques to help teens manage stress, improve focus, and boost self-esteem. Parents will also find tools that will help them to better support their teens and strengthen family bonds.

Technique: Stress-Busting Shield for Teens

Stress is a common issue for teens (and parents of teens), whether it's due to school, relationships, or other factors. Self-hypnosis can help teens relax and reduce stress levels.

Step 1: Make Yourself Comfortable

Find a quiet, comfortable place where you can sit or lie down without being disturbed.

Step 2: Induction and Deepening

Use your favorite induction and deepening technique to enter a relaxed state.

Step 3: Visualizing the Safe Zone

1. **Imagine a Safe Zone**: Picture yourself in a special place where you feel completely safe and at ease. This could be a peaceful beach, a quiet forest, or your favorite room. Visualize the sights, sounds, and smells of this place, and let yourself fully immerse in its tranquility.

Step 4: Creating the Stress-Busting Shield

1. **Imagine a Protective Shield**: Visualize a powerful, glowing shield forming around you. This shield is made of light and energy, designed to protect you from stress. It can be any color you like and has a calming, soothing glow.
2. **Describe the Shield**: Think about how your shield looks. Is it a specific color? Does it have any special designs or symbols? How does it feel to be inside this shield?

Step 5: Using the Shield

1. **Visualize Stressors Bouncing Off**: Picture any stressors you are facing, like exams, social pressures, or family issues, approaching your

shield. See them bouncing off harmlessly, unable to penetrate the protective barrier. Your shield absorbs and neutralizes these stressors, keeping you safe and calm inside.

2. **Feel the Calm**: As the stressors bounce off your shield, feel a sense of calm and relaxation growing inside you. Imagine the shield filling you with positive energy, making you feel stronger and more at ease.

Step 6: Strengthening Your Inner Calm

1. **Visualize Inner Strength**: Picture a warm, glowing light within your chest. This light represents your inner strength and calm. See it growing brighter and stronger with each breath you take, filling your entire body with peace and confidence.

2. **Connect the Shield and Inner Calm**: Imagine your inner light connecting with the shield, creating an unbreakable bond. This connection reinforces your ability to stay calm and stress-free, no matter what challenges you face.

Step 7: Positive Suggestions for Managing Stress

While inside your protective shield, give yourself some positive suggestions to reinforce your ability to manage stress. Repeat these affirmations to yourself:

1. "I am calm and in control."
2. "I can handle any stress that comes my way."
3. "I am strong, confident, and relaxed."
4. "My protective shield keeps me safe and stress-free."
5. "Each day, I grow stronger and more resilient."

Step 8: Returning to Reality

1. **Return from the Visualization**: Imagine gradually returning from your visualization, bringing all the calm and positive energy from the exercise with you. See yourself stepping out of your safe zone but knowing your shield and inner calm stay with you.

2. **Re-enter the Calming Place**: Visualize coming back to your calming place, feeling even more peaceful and confident.

Step 9: Returning to Wakefulness

When you are ready to end the session, imagine leaving your calming place, feeling empowered and stress-free. Count up from one to five. With each count, feel yourself becoming more alert and energized. By the count of five, open your eyes, feeling refreshed and ready to take on the world.

<u>Technique: Improving Focus for Teens</u>

With so many distractions these days, and constantly being bombarded with information, maintaining focus can be challenging for teens. Self-hypnosis can enhance concentration and improve study habits.

Step 1: Make Yourself Comfortable

Find a quiet, comfortable place where you can sit or lie down without being disturbed.

Step 2: Induction and Deepening

Use your favorite induction and deepening technique to enter a relaxed state.

Step 3: Visualizing the Focus Room

1. **Imagine the Focus Room**: Picture yourself entering a special room designed for ultimate focus and concentration. This room can be anything you want. Visualize the sights, sounds, and smells of this place, and let yourself fully immerse in it.

Step 4: Creating the Laser Focus Light

1. **Imagine a Beam of Light**: Visualize a powerful beam of light coming from above, shining down into the center of your focus room. This light is your "Laser Focus Light," and it helps you concentrate on whatever task you need to do.
2. **Describe the Light:** Think about how your Laser Focus Light looks. Is it a specific color? How bright is it? How does it make you feel when it shines on you?

Step 5: Using the Laser Focus Light

1. **Visualize the Light Shining on Your Task**: Picture yourself sitting in

your focus room with the task you need to concentrate on in front of you. This could be studying for an exam, doing homework, or practicing a skill. Imagine the Laser Focus Light shining directly on your task, illuminating it and making everything else fade into the background.

2. **Feel the Concentration:** As the Laser Focus Light shines on your task, feel a sense of clarity and concentration growing inside you. Imagine any distractions fading away, unable to penetrate the beam of light. Your mind becomes sharp and focused.

Step 6: Strengthening Your Focus

1. **Visualize Inner Clarity:** Picture a glowing light within your mind, representing your inner clarity and focus. See it growing brighter and more focused with each breath you take, filling your mind with sharpness and concentration.

2. **Connect the Light and Inner Clarity**: Imagine your inner light connecting with the Laser Focus Light, creating a powerful bond. This connection reinforces your ability to stay focused and sharp, no matter what task you are working on.

Step 7: Positive Suggestions for Improving Focus

While inside your focus room and under the Laser Focus Light, give yourself some positive suggestions to reinforce your ability to concentrate. Repeat these affirmations to yourself:

1. "I am focused and attentive."
2. "I can concentrate on any task with ease."
3. "My mind is sharp and clear."
4. "The Laser Focus Light helps me stay on track."
5. "Each day, my concentration improves."

Step 8: Returning to Reality

1. Return from the Visualization: Imagine gradually returning from your visualization, bringing all the clarity and focus from the exercise with you. See yourself stepping out of your focus room but knowing the Laser Focus Light stays with you whenever you need it.
2. Re-enter the Calming Place: Visualize coming back to your calming place, feeling even more focused and confident.

Step 9: Returning to Wakefulness

When you are ready to end the session, imagine leaving your calming place, feeling focused and energized. Count up from one to five. With each count, feel yourself becoming more alert and ready to concentrate. By the count of five, open your eyes, feeling refreshed and ready to tackle your tasks with laser-like focus.

Technique: The Confidence Mirror for Teens

Boosting Self-Esteem

Building self-esteem is crucial for teens as they navigate their formative years. Self-hypnosis can help them develop a positive self-image and increase their confidence.

Step 1: Make Yourself Comfortable

Find a quiet, comfortable place where you can sit or lie down without being disturbed.

Step 2: Induction and Deepening

Use your favorite induction and deepening technique to enter a relaxed state.

Step 3: Visualizing the Confidence Room

1. Imagine the Confidence Room: Picture yourself entering a special room designed to boost your self-esteem. This room can be anything you want—perhaps it's a bright, colorful space filled with your favorite things or a serene, elegant room with soft lighting. Visualize the sights, sounds, and smells of this place, and let yourself fully immerse in its positive energy.

Step 4: Creating the Confidence Mirror

1. **Imagine a Magical Mirror**: Visualize a large, beautiful mirror in the center of your confidence room. This is the Confidence Mirror, and it has the power to reflect all your best qualities and achievements.
2. **Describe the Mirror**: Think about how your Confidence Mirror looks. Is it framed with gold, silver, or bright colors? Does it have any special designs or symbols? How does it make you feel to look into it?

Step 5: Using the Confidence Mirror

1. **Visualize Yourself in the Mirror:** Picture yourself standing in front of the Confidence Mirror. See your reflection smiling back at you, radiating confidence and self-assurance. The mirror highlights all your best features and qualities.
2. **See Your Strengths:** As you look into the mirror, see images of your achievements, talents, and strengths appearing around your reflection. These images remind you of your abilities and accomplishments, reinforcing your self-worth.

Step 6: Embracing Positive Self-Image

1. **Feel the Positive Energy:** Imagine the positive energy from the mirror filling your body, making you feel more confident and self-assured with each breath you take.
2. **Internalize the Positivity:** Picture the positive images and feelings from the mirror becoming a part of you, enhancing your self-esteem and self-image.

Step 7: Positive Suggestions for Self-Esteem

While standing in front of the Confidence Mirror, give yourself some positive suggestions to reinforce your self-esteem. Repeat these affirmations to yourself:

1. "I am confident and capable."
2. "I believe in myself and my abilities."
3. "I am proud of who I am and what I have achieved."
4. "I am worthy of love and respect."
5. "Each day, my confidence grows stronger."

Step 8: Returning to Reality

1. **Return from the Visualization:** Imagine gradually returning from your visualization, bringing all the confidence and positive energy

from the exercise with you. See yourself stepping out of your confidence room but knowing the positive effects of the Confidence Mirror stay with you.

2. **Re-enter the Calming Place:** Visualize coming back to your calming place, feeling even more confident and empowered.

Step 9: Returning to Wakefulness

When you are ready to end the session, imagine leaving your calming place, feeling confident and energized. Count up from one to five. With each count, feel yourself becoming more alert and ready to face the world with renewed self-esteem. By the count of five, open your eyes, feeling refreshed and confident.

<u>Technique: Managing ADD and ADHD for Kids and Teens</u>

Hypnosis offers a unique and effective way to help kids and teens with ADD and ADHD. By using the power of their imagination and focusing their minds, they can improve their attention, control impulsive behaviors, boost their confidence, and develop better organizational skills. It's all about unlocking their potential and giving them the confidence and tools they need to succeed.

If using this for young children where you will be giving the suggestions, there is no need to deepen the trance. Go from the induction right to the visualization.

Step 1: Make Yourself Comfortable

Find a quiet, comfortable place where you can sit or lie down without being disturbed. Ensure the environment is free of distractions.

Step 2: Induction and Deepening

Use your favorite induction and deepening technique to enter a relaxed state.
Step 3: Entering the Visualization

1. **Imagine a Magical Forest**: Picture yourself entering a magical forest filled with enchanting trees, vibrant flowers, and friendly animals. The forest is peaceful and calming, and it makes you feel safe and relaxed. Visualize the sights, sounds, and feelings of this place, and let yourself fully immerse in its soothing energy.
2. **Describe the Forest**: Think about the details of the forest. Are there colorful butterflies, gentle streams, and the soft rustling of leaves? How does it feel to be in this place of tranquility and wonder?

Step 4: Visualizing Focus and Calm

1. **Visualize a Focus Stone**: Imagine finding a special stone in the forest. This stone is called the Focus Stone, and it has magical

properties that help you concentrate and stay calm. See the stone clearly in your mind and notice its unique details. It might be glowing softly and feel warm to the touch.

2. **Describe the Stone**: Think about how this stone looks and feels. Is it smooth, with swirling patterns and a gentle light? How does it feel to hold this Focus Stone in your hand?

Step 5: Using the Focus Stone

1. **Visualize Holding the Stone**: Imagine picking up the Focus Stone and holding it in your hand. Feel its warmth and energy flowing into you, helping you feel more focused and calm.
2. **Feel the Energy**: As you hold the Focus Stone, feel its calming energy spreading throughout your body. Imagine the energy helping you concentrate better and feel more at ease.

Step 6: Applying the Focus and Calm

1. **Visualize a Calm Place in the Forest**: Imagine finding a special spot in the forest where you can sit and relax. This could be a cozy clearing, a soft bed of moss, or a gentle stream. See yourself sitting in this place, feeling calm and focused.
2. **Feel the Calmness and Focus**: As you sit in this calm place, feel the energy from the Focus Stone helping you stay attentive and relaxed. Imagine yourself using this calmness and focus in your daily life, whether it's during school, at home, or with friends.

Step 7: Positive Suggestions for Managing ADD and ADHD

While in your magical forest, give yourself some positive suggestions to reinforce your ability to manage ADD and ADHD. Repeat these affirmations to yourself:

1. "I can focus and stay calm."
2. "I have the ability to concentrate and complete my tasks."

3. "I am in control of my thoughts and actions."
4. "I can use my focus and calm energy whenever I need it."
5. "I am confident in my ability to manage ADD and ADHD."

Step 8: Embracing the Focused and Calm State

1. **Visualize Embracing Your Abilities**: Imagine embracing your body with gratitude and appreciation. Visualize yourself feeling focused, calm, and confident in various situations, whether it's studying, playing, or spending time with family and friends.
2. **Feel the Empowerment**: As you embrace this new state of focus and calm, feel a sense of empowerment and confidence. Know that you have the ability to manage and overcome the challenges of ADD and ADHD.

Step 9: Returning to Reality

1. **Return from the Visualization**: Imagine gradually returning from your visualization, bringing all the focus and calmness from the exercise with you. See yourself leaving the magical forest but knowing the benefits stay with you.
2. **Re-enter the Calming Place**: Visualize coming back to your calming place, feeling even more determined and ready to use your focus and calm energy in your daily life.

Step 10: Returning to Wakefulness

When you are ready to end the session, imagine leaving your calming place, feeling refreshed and empowered. Count up from one to five. With each count, feel yourself becoming more alert and ready to engage in your day. By the count of five, open your eyes, feeling refreshed and in control.

Technique: Calm Oasis for Reducing Parental Stress

Parenting can be stressful, especially during the teenage years. Self-hypnosis can help parents manage their stress and remain calm.

Step 1: Make Yourself Comfortable

Find a quiet, comfortable place where you can sit or lie down without being disturbed. Ensure the environment is free of distractions.

Step 2: Induction and Deepening

Use your favorite induction and deepening technique to enter a relaxed state.

Step 3: Visualizing the Calm Oasis

1. **Imagine the Calm Oasis:** Picture yourself entering a special place designed to reduce your stress and rejuvenate your spirit. This place can be anything you want—a lush garden with flowers, a beautiful beach with gentle waves, or a quiet forest with tall trees. Visualize the sights, sounds, and smells of this place, and let yourself fully immerse in its tranquility.

Step 4: Creating the Relaxation Pool

1. **Imagine a Relaxation Pool:** Visualize a beautiful, calming pool in the center of your oasis. This pool is filled with crystal-clear water that has magical stress-relieving properties.
2. **Describe the Pool:** Think about how your Relaxation Pool looks. Is it surrounded by smooth stones, fragrant flowers, or soft grass? How does it feel to be near it?

Step 5: Using the Relaxation Pool

1. **Visualize Yourself in the Pool:** Picture yourself stepping into the Relaxation Pool. Feel the warm, soothing water surrounding you, washing away all your stress and tension. Imagine yourself floating effortlessly, supported by the calming water.
2. **Feel the Stress Melting Away:** As you float in the pool, feel all your worries and stress dissolving into the water. Visualize the water absorbing your stress, leaving you feeling light and at peace.

Step 6: Embracing Tranquility

1. **Visualize Inner Calm:** Picture a glowing light within your chest, representing your inner calm and peace. See it growing brighter and more soothing with each breath you take, filling your entire body with relaxation.
2. **Connect with Nature:** Imagine the sounds of nature around you—the gentle rustle of leaves, the soft chirping of birds, or the distant sound of waves. Let these sounds enhance your sense of tranquility and connection with your calm oasis.

Step 7: Positive Suggestions for Reducing Stress

While floating in the Relaxation Pool, give yourself some positive suggestions to reinforce your relaxation and stress reduction. Repeat these affirmations to yourself:

1. "I am calm and at peace."
2. "I can handle any challenge with ease."
3. "I deserve this time to relax and rejuvenate."
4. "I am capable and in control."
5. "Each day, I find more moments of peace and relaxation."

Step 8: Returning to Reality

1. **Return from the Visualization:** Imagine gradually returning from your visualization, bringing all the calm and positive energy from the exercise with you. See yourself stepping out of the Relaxation Pool but knowing the tranquility of the oasis stays with you.
2. **Re-enter the Calming Place:** Visualize coming back to your calming place, feeling even more relaxed and rejuvenated.

Step 9: Returning to Wakefulness

When you are ready to end the session, imagine leaving your calming place, feeling refreshed and at peace. Count up from one to five. With each count, feel yourself becoming more alert and ready to face the world with renewed calm. By the count of five, open your eyes, feeling refreshed and stress-free.

Chapter 6.1 Enhancing Communication As a Parent.

Effective communication is key to a healthy parent-teen relationship. Sometimes it can feel like we are beating our heads against a wall, but between the eye rolls, lack of interest, and sometimes looks of disgust, you can still get though, but that often requires us, as parents, to understand that their minds are working differently at this stage of their life, and the way we communicated and directed them in prior years just aren't effective anymore.

When it comes to communicating with your teen, one of the best things you can do is to start asking more questions, rather than talking at them. Self examination is an important part of these years and directing them in using their minds in a better way is one of the best things you can do to help them in the future.

If your teen comes to you with statements like "I'm not smart enough", "I can't do that because_____________", or whatever new beliefs they are beginning to take on that are unhelpful in building them into the best adult possible, ask them "When did you decide that?", "What would you need to do to be able to accomplish that?", "If you could, what would you do next?". Now take that answer and start reframing it. Instead of a problem, reframe it to a challenge, and then ask them if there is a hidden opportunity in this challenge. Get them, and yourself, looking deeper than the "I can't", and "I am" surface-level statements.

One of the most unhelpful ways to help is to respond to statements like "I'm not smart enough" with the typical parental response of, "Of course you are, you are a very smart boy/girl" That may have worked when they were 8, but for a teenager, they won't accept your outright statement.

Self-hypnosis can help parents improve their communication skills by reminding you that it's time to change the way you communicate and hear what they are really trying to say.

Technique: The Bridge of Understanding for Enhanced Communication with Teens

Step 1: Make Yourself Comfortable

Find a quiet, comfortable place where you can sit or lie down without being disturbed. Ensure the environment is welcoming and free of distractions.

Step 2: Induction and Deepening

Use your favorite induction and deepening technique to enter a relaxed state.

Step 3: Visualizing the Bridge of Understanding

1. **Imagine the Bridge**: Picture yourself standing at the edge of a beautiful, sturdy bridge. This bridge represents the connection between you and your teen. It spans a calm river, symbolizing the flow of communication and understanding.
2. **Describe the Bridge**: Think about how your bridge looks. Is it made of stone or wood? Does it have any special features like flowers or lanterns? How does it feel to stand on it?

Step 4: Crossing the Bridge

1. **Visualize Yourself Walking Across:** Imagine yourself walking slowly and confidently across the bridge. With each step, you feel more open and ready to communicate effectively with your teen.
2. **Feel the Connection:** As you walk, feel a sense of connection and understanding growing between you and your teen. Visualize this connection as a glowing light that gets brighter with each step.

Step 5: Meeting Your Teen on the Other Side

1. See Your Teen Waiting: Picture your teen standing on the other side

of the bridge, waiting for you. They are open and ready to communicate with you. Notice their relaxed posture and welcoming expression.

2. Feel the Calm: As you approach your teen, feel a sense of calm and openness. Imagine any barriers to communication dissolving as you get closer.

Step 6: Creating a Safe Space for Communication

1. **Visualize a Safe Circle:** Imagine a safe, magical circle surrounding you and your teen. This circle is filled with trust, respect, and understanding. Inside this circle, both of you feel safe to express your thoughts and feelings.

2. **See the Light of Understanding:** Picture a warm, glowing light in the center of the circle, representing mutual understanding and empathy. This light helps both of you communicate with kindness and clarity.

Step 7: Practicing Effective Communication

1. **Ask Open-Ended Questions:** Visualize yourself asking your teen open-ended questions like, "When did you decide that?" or "What would you need to do to be able to accomplish that?" See your teen responding thoughtfully, engaging in a deeper conversation.

2. **Reframe Challenges:** Imagine your teen expressing a limiting belief like, "I'm not smart enough." Visualize yourself responding by reframing the problem into a challenge and asking, "Is there a hidden opportunity in this challenge?" See your teen considering this new perspective and feeling more empowered.

Step 8: Positive Suggestions for Enhanced Communication

While standing in the safe circle with your teen, give yourself some positive suggestions to reinforce your ability to communicate effectively. Repeat these affirmations to yourself:

1. "I am open and willing to listen."
2. "I communicate with empathy and respect."
3. "I understand and appreciate my teen's perspective."
4. "We express our thoughts and feelings clearly and calmly."
5. "Each day, our communication becomes stronger and more positive."

Step 9: Returning to Reality

1. Return from the Visualization: Imagine gradually returning from your visualization, bringing all the positive energy and understanding from the exercise with you. See yourself walking back across the bridge but knowing the connection and communication with your teen stays strong.
2. Re-enter the Calming Place: Visualize coming back to your calming place, feeling even more confident and connected with your teen.

Step 10: Returning to Wakefulness

When you are ready to end the session, imagine leaving your calming place, feeling refreshed and ready to communicate effectively. Count up from one to five. With each count, feel yourself becoming more alert and ready to engage with your teen. By the count of five, open your eyes, feeling refreshed and connected.

Chapter 6.2: Supporting Teen Success

We obviously all want our children to succeed in life. Whether it is academically, socially, athletically or any other area of their life, the support of a parent is extremely important, but support isn't the same as encouragement or creating false beliefs within them. Supporting their success now means giving them the tools to succeed and flourish, but sometimes, despite our best intentions, we actually can hinder that success. The support you give now could turn into a big barrier to success later in life if it's not pointed in the right direction.

We can actually make their success harder than it needs to be by trying too hard to be their friend instead of a mentor, telling them how great they are rather than helping them overcome and improve shortcomings. Be their friend later in life; the development of their mind in the teen years isn't the time for that. These years are about preparing them, making them strong enough to be independent and confident in their strengths, while recognizing where improvement is needed and showing them the tools to make that improvement. It's crucial to strike a balance between nurturing their self-esteem and instilling a realistic understanding of their abilities and areas for growth.

Today more than ever, so many parents instill in their children this false perception that they are little princes and princesses. Telling them constantly how amazing they are, even when clearly they weren't, makes it always seem that things that go wrong are the fault of someone else or some unfair life circumstance beyond their control. This creates a fragile foundation for their self-worth, one that crumbles easily when faced with real-world challenges. The world is standing by and is going to teach them rather quickly that they are in fact not royalty and far from perfect. When that realization hits them, it can undo everything you thought you were doing to be helpful in these critical teen years. There are no participation awards for adults, and the sooner they learn to handle failure and disappointment, and ways to grow from that failure or disappointment, the better equipped they will be for the future.

Encouraging your kids to take responsibility for their actions, learn from their mistakes, and always strive to get better are some of the most important lessons you can teach them. Instead of just showering them with praise, focus on giving them helpful feedback and guidance. Help them set realistic goals and build the grit to achieve them. Celebrate their efforts and progress, not just the final results. This way, they'll learn the value of hard work and determination, and you'll be setting them up to handle adult life with confidence and skill.

But let's talk about the flip side for a second. Being too critical of your teens can seriously backfire. Constant criticism can really hurt their self-esteem and mental health, leading to feelings of inadequacy, anxiety, and even depression. It can also damage your relationship with them, making them feel alienated and resentful. If they feel like they can never meet your expectations, they might shut down, withdraw, or even rebel.

Instead of harsh criticism, try giving them constructive feedback. Focus on what they can do differently next time. Create an environment where they feel safe to express their thoughts and feelings without worrying about being judged. Listen actively and show that you understand where they're coming from.

Remember, teens are at a stage where they're figuring out who they are and how to navigate the world on their own. Your job is to support and guide them, not to impose unrealistic expectations or be overly critical. Help them see mistakes as chances to learn and grow. Reinforcing that effort and perseverance are way more important than perfection.

By creating a supportive and nurturing environment, you help your teen build a healthy self-image and the confidence to tackle challenges. Encourage them to take risks and try new things, and let them know that making mistakes is just part of the learning process. Teach them problem-solving skills and resilience so they can bounce back from setbacks even stronger.

So, while it's crucial to encourage responsibility and continuous improvement in your teens, it's just as important to avoid being too critical. Aim for a balanced approach that mixes constructive feedback with empathy and support. This way, you'll help your teens grow into well-rounded, resilient, and confident adults who can handle whatever life throws at them.

So then what is the best way to help and support their success?

Parents can use self-hypnosis to support their teens' success in various areas of life, from academics to personal growth.

Technique: The Balanced Support Approach for Parents

Step 1: Make Yourself Comfortable

Find a quiet, comfortable place where you can sit or lie down without being disturbed. Ensure the environment is free of distractions.

Step 2: Induction and Deepening

Use your favorite induction and deepening technique to enter a relaxed state.

Step 3: Visualizing the Path to Success

1. **Imagine the Path**: Picture yourself and your teen standing at the beginning of a beautiful, winding path. This path represents their journey toward success. It's lined with trees, flowers, and milestones that mark their achievements and growth.
2. **Describe the Path**: Think about how this path looks. Is it smooth or a bit rugged? Does it have signs or markers along the way? How does it feel to stand at the beginning of this path with your teen?

Step 4: Walking the Path Together

1. **Visualize Walking with Your Teen**: Imagine yourself walking alongside your teen on this path. With each step, feel the connection and support growing between you. Your role is to guide, support, and encourage them without taking over.
2. **Feel the Connection**: As you walk, feel a sense of balance and understanding. You're there to help them navigate obstacles, but you also allow them to make their own decisions and learn from their experiences.

Step 5: Providing Balanced Support

1. **Visualize Encouragement and Guidance**: Picture moments along the path where your teen faces challenges or makes mistakes. See yourself offering balanced support—providing constructive feedback, asking insightful questions, and helping them find their own solutions. Instead of saying, "You're amazing," you might ask, "What did you learn from this?" or "How can you improve next time?"
2. **Recognize Achievements**: Imagine celebrating your teen's efforts and progress, not just the end results. See yourself acknowledging their hard work, resilience, and growth. This reinforces the value of persistence and improvement.

Step 6: Practicing Empathy and Constructive Feedback

1. **Visualize Empathetic Listening**: Picture a moment where your teen expresses frustration or self-doubt. See yourself listening attentively, showing empathy, and validating their feelings. This creates a safe space for open communication.
2. **Offer Constructive Feedback**: Visualize giving feedback that focuses on improvement without harsh criticism. For example, instead of saying, "You should have done better," say, "What can you do differently next time to improve?" This approach encourages learning and growth.

Step 7: Positive Suggestions for Supportive Parenting

While walking the path with your teen, give yourself some positive suggestions to reinforce your supportive parenting approach. Repeat these affirmations to yourself:

1. "I provide balanced support and guidance."
2. "I help my teen learn from their experiences."
3. "I celebrate my teen's efforts and progress."
4. "I offer empathy and constructive feedback."

5. "I am a guide and mentor, helping my teen build resilience and confidence."

Step 8: Returning to Reality

1. **Return from the Visualization**: Imagine gradually returning from your visualization, bringing all the positive energy and understanding from the exercise with you. See yourself and your teen continuing on the path to success, knowing you are there to support them in the right way.
2. **Re-enter the Calming Place:** Visualize coming back to your calming place, feeling even more confident and balanced in your approach to supporting your teen.

Step 9: Returning to Wakefulness

When you are ready to end the session, imagine leaving your calming place, feeling refreshed and ready to support your teen effectively. Count up from one to five. With each count, feel yourself becoming more alert and ready to engage with your teen. By the count of five, open your eyes, feeling refreshed and connected.

Chapter 7: Boosting Sports Performance

Whether you're an athlete or just enjoy staying active, self-hypnosis can enhance your performance. We'll look at techniques to improve concentration, overcome performance anxiety, and visualize success.

A lot of professional athletes have publicly acknowledged using hypnosis or hypnotherapy to enhance their performance. Here are a few examples:

1. **Tiger Woods** - Even with his recent physical setbacks, Tiger Woods has been a big believer in hypnosis and mental conditioning. He started young, using these techniques to sharpen his focus and stay mentally tough. Hypnosis has helped him visualize those perfect shots, keep his cool under pressure, and bounce back from tough times. This mental edge has been key to his amazing golf career.

2. **Michael Jordan** - The basketball legend used visualization, which is kind of like hypnosis, to get ready for games and boost his performance. By picturing himself making clutch shots and great plays, Jordan could mentally rehearse and build confidence before hitting the court. This helped him stay calm, focused, and at the top of his game, even when the stakes were high.

3. **Phil Jackson** - While he wasn't an athlete, Phil Jackson, the famous NBA coach, used hypnosis-like techniques with his teams, like the Chicago Bulls and LA Lakers. He got players like Michael Jordan and Kobe Bryant into mindfulness, meditation, and visualization exercises to improve their mental game. This helped them stay focused, manage stress, and play better overall.

4. **Steve Hooker** - The Olympic pole vaulter has talked openly about using hypnosis to get over a mental block and succeed in his sport. Hooker used hypnosis to visualize his vaults and keep a calm, focused mindset during competitions. This mental training helped him overcome his fears and anxieties, leading to his gold medal at the 2008 Beijing Olympics.

5. **Mike Tyson** - The former boxing champ used hypnosis as part of his training. His hypnosis sessions focused on building a strong, focused mindset, boosting his confidence, and visualizing success in the ring. This mental prep was key to Tyson's fierce dominance in boxing.

6. **Jimmy Connors** - This tennis champ credited hypnosis for helping him stay focused and improve his game. Connors used hypnosis to visualize his matches, concentrate better, and stay mentally tough during big moments. These techniques helped him play consistently well and have a long, successful career.

7. **Wayne Gretzky** - The hockey legend used visualization and mental training, often linked to hypnosis, to up his game on the ice. Gretzky would mentally rehearse plays, anticipate opponents' moves, and visualize successful shots. This mental prep kept him ahead of the competition and performing with amazing precision and confidence.

8. **Andre Agassi** - The tennis star reportedly used hypnosis to help with focus and mental toughness during matches. Agassi's hypnosis sessions involved visualizing his serves, groundstrokes, and winning points. This mental rehearsal helped him stay calm, focused, and resilient, even in the most intense matches, contributing to his Grand Slam wins.

9. **Ken Norton** - The boxer used hypnosis to get ready for his fights, including his famous win over Muhammad Ali. Norton's hypnosis training involved visualizing successful punches, defensive moves, and fight strategies. This mental conditioning built his confidence, kept him focused, and helped him execute his game plan effectively, leading to his historic victory over Ali.

Let's look at some specific techniques and suggestions to help you perform at your absolute best.

Technique: Power-Up Visualization for Boosting Sports Performance

Step 1: Make Yourself Comfortable

Find a quiet, comfortable place where you can sit or lie down without being disturbed.

Step 2: Induction and Deepening

Use your favorite induction and deepening technique to enter a relaxed state.

Step 3: Visualizing the Power-Up Zone

1. **Imagine the Power-Up Zone:** Picture yourself entering a special zone designed to enhance your sports performance. This zone can be anything you want— a cutting-edge training facility, a natural environment, or a grand stadium. Visualize the sights, sounds, and smells of this place, and let yourself fully immerse in its energy.

Step 4: Creating the Performance Amplifier

1. **Imagine a Powerful Source:** Visualize a powerful, glowing source of energy in the center of your Power-Up Zone. This source represents all the strength, focus, and endurance you need to perform at your best.
2. **Describe the Source:** Think about how your Performance Amplifier looks. Is it a specific color? How bright is it? How does it make you feel when it shines on you?

Step 5: Using the Performance Amplifier

1. **Visualize Yourself in Action:** Picture yourself performing your sport at your peak. See every detail—your movements, your posture, and

your focus. Imagine the Performance Amplifier energizing you, enhancing your abilities and concentration.

2. **Feel the Power and Confidence**: As the Performance Amplifier energizes you, feel a surge of power, confidence, and determination. Imagine any doubts or fears dissolving away, replaced by a sense of mastery and control.

Step 6: Embracing Peak Performance

1. **Visualize Success**: Picture yourself successfully completing a key aspect of your sport—whether it's scoring a goal, making a perfect shot, or executing a flawless routine. See it clearly in your mind and feel the triumph of achieving it.
2. **Feel the Flow**: Imagine yourself in a state of flow, where everything feels effortless and natural. Visualize yourself moving with ease and precision, fully immersed in the moment.

Step 7: Positive Suggestions for Peak Performance

While in your Power-Up Zone and energized by the Performance Amplifier, give yourself some positive suggestions to reinforce your peak performance. Repeat these affirmations to yourself:

1. "I am powerful and confident."
2. "I perform at my best with ease and precision."
3. "I have the strength and energy to succeed."
4. "I am in the zone, fully immersed in my sport."
5. "Each day, my performance improves and I achieve my goals."

Step 8: Returning to Reality

1. **Return from the Visualization**: Imagine gradually returning from your visualization, bringing all the power and confidence from the exercise with you. See yourself leaving the Power-Up Zone but knowing the benefits stay with you.

2. **Re-enter the Calming Place**: Visualize coming back to your calming place, feeling even more focused and ready for peak performance.

Step 9: Returning to Wakefulness

When you are ready to end the session, imagine leaving your calming place, feeling energized and prepared to perform at your best. Count up from one to five. With each count, feel yourself becoming more alert and ready to engage in your sport. By the count of five, open your eyes, feeling refreshed and confident.

Technique: Calm Champion Visualization for Overcoming Sports Performance Anxiety

Step 1: Make Yourself Comfortable

Find a quiet, comfortable place where you can sit or lie down without being disturbed.

Step 2: Induction and Deepening

Use your favorite induction and deepening technique to enter a relaxed state.

Step 3: Visualizing the Calm Champion Zone

1. **Imagine the Calm Champion Zone**: Picture yourself entering a special zone designed to help you stay calm and focused during sports performance. This zone can be anything you want—perhaps it's a serene natural environment, a peaceful beach, or a quiet training facility. Visualize the sights, sounds, and smells of this place, and let yourself fully immerse in its tranquility.

Step 4: Creating the Calm Shield

1. **Imagine a Protective Shield**: Visualize a powerful, glowing shield around you. This shield represents calmness, confidence, and focus, protecting you from anxiety and negative thoughts.
2. **Describe the Shield**: Think about how your Calm Shield looks. Is it a specific color? How bright is it? How does it make you feel when it surrounds you?

Step 5: Using the Calm Shield

1. **Visualize Yourself in Action**: Picture yourself performing your sport with complete calmness and confidence. See every detail—your

movements, your posture, and your focus. Imagine the Calm Shield surrounding you, keeping you protected from any anxiety or distractions.

2. **Feel the Calm and Confidence**: As the Calm Shield surrounds you, feel a wave of calmness, confidence, and focus washing over you. Imagine any doubts or fears dissolving away, replaced by a sense of control and clarity.

Step 6: Embracing Peak Performance

1. **Visualize Success**: Picture yourself successfully completing a key aspect of your sport—whether it's scoring a goal, making a perfect shot, or executing a flawless routine. See it clearly in your mind and feel the triumph of achieving it.
2. **Feel the Flow**: Imagine yourself in a state of flow, where everything feels effortless and natural. Visualize yourself moving with ease and precision, fully immersed in the moment.

Step 7: Positive Suggestions for Overcoming Anxiety

While in your Calm Champion Zone and surrounded by the Calm Shield, give yourself some positive suggestions to reinforce your ability to stay calm and focused. Repeat these affirmations to yourself:

1. "I am calm and confident."
2. "I perform at my best with ease and focus."
3. "I am in control of my thoughts and emotions."
4. "I am protected by my Calm Shield."
5. "Each day, my confidence and performance improve."

Step 8: Returning to Reality

1. **Return from the Visualization**: Imagine gradually returning from your visualization, bringing all the calmness and confidence from the exercise with you. See yourself leaving the Calm Champion Zone but

knowing the benefits stay with you.

2. **Re-enter the Calming Place**: Visualize coming back to your calming place, feeling even more focused and ready for peak performance.

Step 9: Returning to Wakefulness

When you are ready to end the session, imagine leaving your calming place, feeling calm and prepared to perform at your best. Count up from one to five. With each count, feel yourself becoming more alert and ready to engage in your sport. By the count of five, open your eyes, feeling refreshed and confident.

Technique: Muscle Growth and Strength Visualization

Step 1: Make Yourself Comfortable

Find a quiet, comfortable place where you can sit or lie down without being disturbed.

Step 2: Induction and Deepening

Use your favorite induction and deepening technique to enter a relaxed state.

Step 3: Visualizing the Inner Gym

1. **Imagine the Inner Gym**: Picture yourself entering a state-of-the-art gym, designed specifically to enhance muscle growth and increase strength. This gym is equipped with the latest fitness equipment and has a vibrant, energetic atmosphere. Visualize the sights, sounds, and smells of this place, and let yourself fully immerse in its empowering energy.
2. **Describe the Gym**: Think about the details of the gym. Is it filled with natural light, surrounded by motivational posters, or equipped with advanced training machines? How does it feel to be in this powerful, motivating place?

Step 4: Creating the Muscle-Enhancing Energy

1. **Imagine a Powerful Energy Source**: Visualize a powerful, glowing source of energy in the center of the gym. This energy represents all the strength, endurance, and growth needed to enhance your muscles.
2. **Describe the Energy**: Think about how your Muscle-Enhancing Energy looks. Is it a specific color? How bright is it? How does it make you feel when it energizes you?

Step 5: Using the Muscle-Enhancing Energy

1. **Visualize Yourself in Action**: Picture yourself working out in the gym, performing various exercises such as lifting weights, doing push-ups, or squats. See every detail—your movements, your posture, and your focus. Imagine the Muscle-Enhancing Energy infusing every muscle, enhancing your strength and growth.
2. **Feel the Growth and Strength**: As the Muscle-Enhancing Energy flows through you, feel a surge of power, endurance, and confidence. Imagine your muscles growing stronger and more defined with each exercise, any fatigue dissolving away, replaced by a sense of capability and growth.

Step 6: Embracing Muscle Growth and Strength

1. **Visualize Muscle Development**: Picture your muscles becoming more defined and powerful. See them growing and strengthening with each exercise. Visualize your body transforming into a stronger, more resilient version of itself.
2. **Feel the Strength**: Imagine yourself feeling strong and powerful, with every muscle in your body working efficiently and effectively. Visualize yourself moving with ease and precision, fully immersed in the moment.

Step 7: Positive Suggestions for Muscle Growth

While in your Inner Gym and energized by the Muscle-Enhancing Energy, give yourself some positive suggestions to reinforce your muscle growth and strength. Repeat these affirmations to yourself:

1. "My muscles are growing stronger every day."
2. "I am capable of achieving my strength goals."
3. "I have the power and endurance to enhance my physique."
4. "I am energized and powerful."
5. "Each day, my muscles become more defined and resilient."

Step 8: Returning to Reality

1. **Return from the Visualization**: Imagine gradually returning from your visualization, bringing all the strength and energy from the exercise with you. See yourself leaving the Inner Gym but knowing the benefits stay with you.
2. **Re-enter the Calming Place**: Visualize coming back to your calming place, feeling even more focused and ready for muscle growth and strength.

Step 9: Returning to Wakefulness

When you are ready to end the session, imagine leaving your calming place, feeling strong and prepared to enhance your physical abilities. Count up from one to five. With each count, feel yourself becoming more alert and ready to engage in your physical activities. By the count of five, open your eyes,

Chapter 8: Academic Excellence

Self-hypnosis is a powerful tool for boosting academic performance. Whether you're a student struggling with test anxiety, finding it hard to concentrate, or looking to improve your memory, self-hypnosis can be your secret weapon. In this chapter, we'll explore how students can use self-hypnosis to enhance their academic performance and make studying more effective and enjoyable.

There are 3 primary areas where using self-hypnosis can give you the biggest benefit in improving academic performance. My first exposure to hypnosis as a child was to improve my own performance in elementary school.

Improving Memory

One of the key benefits of self-hypnosis is its ability to improve memory. By entering a relaxed, focused state, you can enhance your brain's ability to encode and retrieve information. This technique is similar to what Albert Einstein practiced. He was known to use visualization techniques, which are a form of self-hypnosis, to solve complex problems and retain vast amounts of information.

PERSONAL TRANSFORMATION FROM WITHIN: THE POWER OF SELF HYPNOSIS FOR LASTING CHANGE

Enhancing Concentration

Concentration is crucial for effective studying, and self-hypnosis can help students maintain focus for longer periods. By practicing self-hypnosis regularly, students can train their minds to block out distractions and stay engaged with their work. Thomas Edison, the inventor, reportedly used self-hypnosis to help him focus and think more creatively. He would enter a state of deep relaxation to come up with new ideas and solutions.

Managing Test Anxiety

Test anxiety can be a problem for a lot of students, but self-hypnosis offers an effective way to overcome it. By using self-hypnosis techniques, students can calm their minds and bodies, reducing the overwhelming feelings of stress that often come with exams. With regular practice, self-hypnosis helps students stay composed and clear-headed during tests, allowing them to recall information more effectively and perform at their best. This approach not only makes test-taking less stressful but also boosts overall academic performance.

Technique: Memory Garden Visualization for Academic Success

Step 1: Make Yourself Comfortable

Find a quiet, comfortable place where you can sit or lie down without being disturbed.

Step 2: Induction and Deepening

Use your favorite induction and deepening technique to enter a relaxed state.

Step 3: Visualizing the Memory Garden

1. **Imagine the Memory Garden**: Picture yourself entering a tranquil, inspiring garden designed to enhance your memory and academic success. This garden is filled with vibrant flowers, shady trees, and unique plants, each holding specific information you need to remember. Visualize the sights, sounds, and smells of this place, and let yourself fully immerse in its calm, focused energy.
2. **Describe the Garden**: Think about the details of the garden. Is it filled with colorful flowers, surrounded by gentle streams, or adorned with inspiring sculptures? How does it feel to be in this place of learning and focus?

Step 4: Creating the Knowledge Plants

1. **Imagine Knowledge Plants**: Visualize each flower, tree, or plant in the garden as a holder of specific information. Each one is unique and represents a different subject or topic you need to remember. For example, a vibrant sunflower might hold the key points from a history lesson, while a tall oak tree might contain important formulas for a math exam.
2. **Describe the Plants**: Think about how each plant looks. What colors

are they? What type of plants are they? How does each one make you feel when you look at them?

Step 5: Using the Knowledge Plants

1. **Visualize Yourself Studying**: Picture yourself in a study area within the garden, surrounded by the Knowledge Plants. See every detail—your posture, your concentration, and your focus. Imagine walking through the garden, touching each plant, and absorbing the specific information it holds.
2. **Feel the Clarity and Focus**: As you interact with the plants, feel a surge of clarity, focus, and confidence. Imagine any distractions or doubts dissolving away, replaced by a sense of understanding and retention.

Step 6: Embracing Academic Success

1. **Visualize Academic Achievements**: Picture yourself successfully remembering and applying the things you have learned. See yourself acing exams, writing perfect essays, or being confident in class discussions. Visualize the sense of accomplishment and satisfaction that comes with this success.
2. **Feel the Success**: Imagine yourself feeling confident and capable, with every study session and class enhancing your academic performance. Visualize yourself moving through your studies with ease and precision, fully immersed in the learning process.

Step 7: Positive Suggestions for Memory Improvement

While in your Memory Garden and interacting with the Knowledge Plants, give yourself some positive suggestions to reinforce your memory and academic success. Repeat these affirmations to yourself:

1. "My memory is sharp and reliable."
2. "I easily retain and recall information."

3. "I am confident in my academic abilities."
4. "I am focused and attentive while studying."
5. "Each day, my memory and understanding improve."

Step 8: Returning to Reality

1. **Return from the Visualization**: Imagine gradually returning from your visualization, bringing all the clarity and focus from the exercise with you. See yourself leaving the Memory Garden but knowing the benefits stay with you.
2. **Re-enter the Calming Place**: Visualize coming back to your calming place, feeling even more focused and ready for academic success.

Step 9: Returning to Wakefulness

When you are ready to end the session, imagine leaving your calming place, feeling clear-minded and prepared to excel in your studies. Count up from one to five. With each count, feel yourself becoming more alert and ready to engage in your academic activities. By the count of five, open your eyes, feeling refreshed and confident.

Technique: The Focus Forest Visualization for Enhancing Concentration

Step 1: Make Yourself Comfortable

Find a quiet, comfortable place where you can sit or lie down without being disturbed. Ensure the environment is welcoming and free of distractions.

Step 2: Induction and Deepening

Use your favorite induction and deepening technique to enter a relaxed state. This might involve deep breathing, progressive muscle relaxation, or imagining a peaceful place. Allow yourself to relax deeply and completely.

Step 3: Visualizing the Focus Forest

1. **Imagine the Focus Forest**: Picture yourself entering a serene and enchanting forest designed to enhance your concentration and academic success. This forest is filled with tall trees, gentle streams, and lush greenery, creating an atmosphere of tranquility and focus. Visualize the sights, sounds, and smells of this place, and let yourself fully immerse in its calming, focused energy.
2. **Describe the Forest**: Think about the details of the forest. Are there specific trees that stand out? Can you hear birds singing or the rustling of leaves? How does it feel to be in this place of deep concentration and peace?

Step 4: Creating the Focus Stream

1. **Imagine a Gentle Stream**: Visualize a clear, flowing stream in the center of your Focus Forest. This stream represents clarity, focus, and the ability to concentrate on your studies effortlessly. The water flowing from the stream is pure and sparkling, symbolizing a clear and focused mind.
2. **Describe the Stream**: Think about how your Focus Stream looks. Is it surrounded by rocks, flowers, or ferns? How does it make you feel when you see and hear the water flowing?

Step 5: Using the Focus Stream

1. **Visualize Yourself Studying**: Picture yourself in a comfortable study area within the forest, near the Focus Stream. See every detail—your posture, your concentration, and your focus. Imagine the sound of the stream enhancing your ability to concentrate and stay focused on your tasks.
2. **Feel the Clarity and Focus**: As you listen to the soothing sound of the water, feel a surge of clarity, focus, and determination. Imagine any distractions or doubts dissolving away, replaced by a sense of

understanding and concentration.

Step 6: Embracing Academic Success

1. **Visualize Academic Achievements**: Picture yourself successfully concentrating on and completing your academic tasks. See yourself reading, writing, and studying with complete focus and efficiency. Visualize the sense of accomplishment and satisfaction that comes with achieving your academic goals.
2. **Feel the Success**: Imagine yourself feeling confident and capable, with every study session and class enhancing your concentration and academic performance. Visualize yourself moving through your studies with ease and precision, fully immersed in the learning process.

Step 7: Positive Suggestions for Enhancing Concentration

While in your Focus Forest and near the Focus Stream, give yourself some positive suggestions to reinforce your concentration and academic success. Repeat these affirmations to yourself:

1. "My concentration is strong and unwavering."
2. "I easily focus on my studies and tasks."
3. "I am confident in my ability to concentrate and succeed academically."
4. "I am calm, clear, and focused while studying."
5. "Each day, my concentration and understanding improve."

Step 8: Returning to Reality

1. **Return from the Visualization**: Imagine gradually returning from your visualization, bringing all the clarity and focus from the exercise with you. See yourself leaving the Focus Forest but knowing the benefits stay with you.
2. **Re-enter the Calming Place**: Visualize coming back to your calming

place, feeling even more focused and ready for academic success.

Step 9: Returning to Wakefulness

When you are ready to end the session, imagine leaving your calming place, feeling clear-minded and prepared to excel in your studies. Count up from one to five. With each count, feel yourself becoming more alert and ready to engage in your academic activities. By the count of five, open your eyes, feeling refreshed and confident.

Technique: The Test Confidence Visualization for Managing Test Anxiety

Step 1: Make Yourself Comfortable

Find a quiet, comfortable place where you can sit or lie down without being disturbed.

Step 2: Induction and Deepening

Use your favorite induction and deepening technique to enter a relaxed state.

Step 3: Visualizing the Test Confidence Room

1. **Imagine the Test Confidence Room**: Picture yourself entering a serene and empowering room designed to boost your confidence and calm your nerves for test-taking. This room is filled with soft lighting, comfortable furniture, and an atmosphere of peace and focus. Visualize the sights, sounds, and smells of this place, and let yourself fully immerse in its calming, confident energy.
2. **Describe the Room**: Think about the details of the room. Are there calming colors on the walls, motivational quotes, or serene landscapes? How does it feel to be in this place of confidence and peace?

Step 4: Creating the Calm Fountain

1. **Imagine a Calm Fountain**: Visualize a gentle, flowing fountain in the center of your Test Confidence Room. This fountain represents calmness, clarity, and the ability to manage test anxiety effortlessly. The water flowing from the fountain is clear and soothing, symbolizing a clear and relaxed mind.
2. **Describe the Fountain**: Think about how your Calm Fountain looks. Is it surrounded by plants, stones, or candles? How does it

make you feel when you see and hear the water flowing?

Step 5: Using the Calm Fountain

1. **Visualize Yourself Studying and Taking the Test**: Picture yourself sitting at a desk in the Test Confidence Room, preparing for an upcoming test. See every detail—your posture, your concentration, and your calm demeanor. Imagine the sound of the fountain enhancing your ability to absorb information and stay relaxed.
2. **Feel the Calm and Confidence**: As you listen to the soothing sound of the water, feel a surge of calmness, clarity, and confidence. Imagine any anxiety or doubts dissolving away, replaced by a sense of peace and readiness.

Step 6: Embracing Test Success

1. **Visualize Test Success**: Picture yourself successfully taking the test with confidence and ease. See yourself reading each question, recalling the information effortlessly, and answering accurately. Visualize the sense of accomplishment and satisfaction that comes with doing well on the test.
2. **Feel the Success**: Imagine yourself feeling confident and capable, with every study session and test enhancing your academic performance. Visualize yourself moving through the test with ease and precision, fully immersed in the process.

Step 7: Positive Suggestions for Managing Test Anxiety

While in your Test Confidence Room and near the Calm Fountain, give yourself some positive suggestions to reinforce your calmness and confidence. Repeat these affirmations to yourself:

1. "I am calm and confident during tests."
2. "I easily recall information and answer questions accurately."
3. "I am well-prepared and capable of succeeding."

4. "I am relaxed and focused while taking tests."
5. "Each day, my confidence and test-taking abilities improve."

Step 8: Returning to Reality

1. **Return from the Visualization**: Imagine gradually returning from your visualization, bringing all the calmness and confidence from the exercise with you. See yourself leaving the Test Confidence Room but knowing the benefits stay with you.
2. **Re-enter the Calming Place**: Visualize coming back to your calming place, feeling even more focused and ready for test success.

Step 9: Returning to Wakefulness

When you are ready to end the session, imagine leaving your calming place, feeling clear-minded and prepared to excel in your tests. Count up from one to five. With each count, feel yourself becoming more alert and ready to engage in your academic activities. By the count of five, open your eyes, feeling refreshed and confident.

<u>Technique: The Personalized Study Haven Visualization</u>

Step 1: Make Yourself Comfortable

Find a quiet, comfortable place where you can sit or lie down without being disturbed.

Step 2: Induction and Deepening

Use your favorite induction and deepening technique to enter a relaxed state.

Step 3: Visualizing Your Personalized Study Haven

1. **Imagine Your Ideal Study Haven**: Picture yourself entering a place designed to make studying enjoyable and effective. This haven can be anything you want—it can be a serene garden, a library, a sunny beach, or a mountain retreat. Visualize the sights, sounds, and smells of this place, and let yourself fully immerse in its uplifting, motivating energy.
2. **Describe Your Haven**: Think about the details of your study haven. What elements make it perfect for you? Are there flowers, trees, bookshelves, or the sound of waves? How does it feel to be in this place of learning and enjoyment?

Step 4: Creating the Inspiration Source

1. **Imagine an Inspiration Source**: Visualize a central element in your study haven that represents inspiration, focus, and the joy of learning. This could be a flowing fountain, a glowing lantern, a crackling fire, or any other feature that symbolizes a clear and motivated mind.
2. **Describe the Source**: Think about how your Inspiration Source looks and feels. Is it surrounded by nature, cozy furniture, or calming colors? How does it make you feel when you see and hear it?

Step 5: Using the Inspiration Source

1. **Visualize Yourself Studying**: Picture yourself in a comfortable study spot within your haven, near your Inspiration Source. See every detail—your posture, your concentration, and your enjoyment of the learning process. Imagine the presence of your Inspiration Source enhancing your focus and making studying a pleasant experience.
2. **Feel the Enjoyment and Motivation**: As you connect with your Inspiration Source, feel a surge of enjoyment, motivation, and clarity. Imagine any boredom or reluctance dissolving away, replaced by a sense of excitement and curiosity.

Step 6: Embracing the Joy of Learning

1. **Visualize Successful Study Sessions**: Picture yourself engaging deeply with your study materials, feeling intrigued and inspired by the information. See yourself taking notes, solving problems, and making connections with ease and enthusiasm. Visualize the sense of accomplishment and satisfaction that comes with enjoyable, productive study sessions.
2. **Feel the Success**: Imagine yourself feeling confident and capable, with every study session enhancing your academic performance and enjoyment of learning. Visualize yourself moving through your studies with ease and joy, fully immersed in the process.

Step 7: Positive Suggestions for Enjoyable Studying

While in your Personalized Study Haven and near your Inspiration Source, give yourself some positive suggestions to reinforce your enjoyment of studying. Repeat these affirmations to yourself:

1. "I enjoy studying and learning new things."
2. "I am curious and motivated while studying."
3. "I find joy and satisfaction in the learning process."
4. "I am focused and engaged during my study sessions."

5. "Each day, my love for learning grows stronger."

Step 8: Returning to Reality

1. **Return from the Visualization**: Imagine gradually returning from your visualization, bringing all the enjoyment and motivation from the exercise with you. See yourself leaving your Personalized Study Haven but knowing the benefits stay with you.
2. **Re-enter the Calming Place**: Visualize coming back to your calming place, feeling even more focused and ready to enjoy your studies.

Step 9: Returning to Wakefulness

When you are ready to end the session, imagine leaving your calming place, feeling refreshed and excited to study. Count up from one to five. With each count, feel yourself becoming more alert and ready to engage in your academic activities. By the count of five, open your eyes, feeling refreshed and motivated.

Chapter 9: Overcoming Anxiety and Depression

Anxiety and depression are common challenges for a lot of people, but hypnosis as well as self-hypnosis offers a way to manage these conditions, but first let's talk more about anxiety and depression, where it comes from, and some other tools that can help you overcome them.

While anxiety and depression are different, they share a common theme, and that theme is that they are both tied to an irrational thought that has taken on a life of itself. There is almost always an initial root cause for the anxiety or depression and the mind has taken that thought or experience and in an attempt to protect you, it keeps your sympathetic nervous system engaged. That sympathetic nervous system is responsible for your fight, flight, or freeze response to danger. When it activates that response it also floods your body with stress hormones and chemicals. Being in a state where your sympathetic nervous system is always in an activated state can lead to a lot of problems in life, both mentally and physically.

Earlier in the book I talked about how the subconscious mind can't tell the difference between past, present, and future and how it doesn't know what's real and what's imagined. It thinks everything is happening now. When an irrational thought pops into our mind, the mind goes forward or backward in time to where that irrational thought resides and thinks that the danger is real and happening at the moment. Once that connection is made, the sympathetic nervous system is activated and the cycle begins. That cycle might include physical sensations that you feel in the stomach, chest, or other area of your body. Your breathing depth and rate change, your physiology likely changes, and your thinking and focus often become irrational and cloudy. Then perhaps you try and fight it, to try and push it away only to find that the harder you try and push, the harder it pushes back. You try to calm yourself only to find that the negative feelings and thoughts intensify.

Anxiety and depression become more than a mind challenge alone, they become a physical issue as your mind throws all of its resources at you all at once. Again, to the mind, it's thinking it's protecting you from danger.

When you try and push it away you bring your focus to it. When you bring your focus to the negative thoughts and emotions, you often get more of them.

Tony Robbins, who is one of the best-known empowerment coaches in the world, coined the term "the triad" when describing emotional states, and how we have the ability to change our state almost instantly from negative to positive.

The triad is made up of 3 components. Focus, Physiology, and Language. While these components are rooted in cognitive behavior therapy and other modalities, Tony has a way of presenting complex ideas in a way that is accessible and actionable for a broader audience, which is a big part of his success in helping people empower themselves.

Let's look at each component. First, there is focus. At the first sign of feeling depression or anxiety showing up at your doorstep, what's the first thing you do? You turn your focus to it. It would be unusual if you didn't.

Now in most cases, there is usually a physiological change that happens which is the second component. For depression you probably hang your head, breathing becomes shallow, and your posture or shoulders may slump forward. For those dealing with anxiety, your chest may tighten, breathing changes and the way you hold your body is the exact opposite of relaxed and calm.

Then we have the language we use. "I'm so depressed", "I'm having an anxiety attack". Whatever you're feeling you likely use language that goes right to the most extreme words that you have available.

Now that the triad is complete, you certainly are depressed or anxious. How could you not be? You have the focus, physiology, and language of a depressed or anxious person. You've given your mind clear instruction that you are depressed or anxious so the mind creates more of those thoughts, it creates all of those unwanted physical sensations, and it releases the corresponding chemicals and hormones.

It's by recognizing and using all of the tools available to us that we can begin changing our experience permanently.

First, we change the triad and create a new state. The first change is in our focus. In the techniques that follow you will be anchoring good feelings and emotions from the past and focusing on those. So to change your focus you will activate the anchor and turn your focus to calm, happy, relaxed, grateful, or love. We will change it to anything other than depression, anxiety, or any other negative state of feeling.

Now you will change your physiology. Stand up straight, breathe deeper, hold your head straight, and smile. I don't care if you are faking it, if your focus is on something good and happy and your body matches that, it's really hard for your mind to keep pumping out those chemicals and hormones because your state doesn't match that of a depressed or anxious person.

Now comes the final ingredient, Language. Instead of saying "I'm so depressed", change your language to something along the lines of "I'm feeling **a little down** today, but I know it will pass". Instead of "I'm having an anxiety attack", change it to something like, "Even though I'm feeling **a little nervous**, I know everything is fine and it will pass quickly". The language we use in our internal communication is extremely important. The more intense you make it, the more intense you will feel it.

Now that you changed the elements of the state, go into self-hypnosis to let it go completely.

There may be times that these negative states hit so fast and so intensely that it can be hard to not let it consume you. In those cases I have clients do one simple thing. Give the mind more than it wants, or expects. Make it so that the mind realizes that it isn't needed at the moment and that you are consciously in control.

For anxiety, if you normally feel tense all over when it arrives, intentionally tighten every muscle in your body as much as you can and hold your breath for about 5 seconds. Make it intense. Make your mind say "What are you doing?!?, Calm down!!". After that 5 seconds, rapidly release the breath, let your body completely relax, and slump down. Imagine that all of the stress and tension left you with that release of the breath. Now that it's gone it can be a great time to do a little self-hypnosis deepening and offer suggestions.

For depression, changing state normally helps move you into a better mindset pretty quickly, but there are things you can do to accelerate getting it to leave. We know that depression is almost always linked to a root cause in the past, so we need to intentionally take the mind to the future. That might surprise you that I didn't say something like "ground yourself in the present " like you may have heard in the past. Why would I have you grounded in the present when that's when and where you're feeling depressed? I want you to go past the depressed feelings and zip right to a time when it's gone.

Try this method and see how fast you can feel better. Close your eyes and imagine sitting in a comfortable chair. In front of you, there is a big high definition flat screen TV and the remote is next to you. Create a scene on the television with you as the main character. Picture yourself happy, calm, and confident. Now in a moment you will hit the fast forward button and see the images move by quickly, the scene you create will be of you going from this happy, calm, confident you to a depressed mess and will continue playing in fast forward all the way to a new point of feeling happy, calm, and confident again. This whole scene should only take a few seconds to fast forward from happy, calm, confident to depressed, and back to happy, calm, and confident. Then you'll hit the pause button at the end. I also want you to imagine the version of you on the TV isn't the greatest actor in the world. I want you to see yourself as over the top overly dramatic.

Now after watching that scene zip by, hit the rewind button and see everything playing backward at high speed. Now fast forward again, but add some silly sounds or music to the scene. Rewind again. Hit fast-forward again and make it look like it's an old silent film. Now do it one more time and see yourself at the end completely calm, relaxed, and happy. Zoom in to see yourself smiling, standing up straight, and maybe even taking a bow at the end of the performance. Go ahead and turn the TV off now.

Anxiety and depression can become a habit if it goes on too long. The longer we let it go unresolved you can become anxious over just the thought or worry about feeling anxiety. We can become depressed by thinking about our depression. We create all of these new triggers that often have nothing to do with the root cause of the anxiety or depression.

You can actually become addicted to those stress hormones and chemicals the same way you can become addicted to other substances.

The good news is that through hypnosis, and these other methods, we can have the mind make changes to that response and completely release anxiety and depression permanently.

While anxiety and depression could be a book of their own, these methods have produced some amazing results with my clients.

For additional information on dealing with anxiety and depression, visit https://mindoverthebody.com

Technique: Tranquil Forest Visualization for Calming Anxiety and Depression

Step 1: Make Yourself Comfortable

Find a quiet, comfortable place where you can sit or lie down without being disturbed.

Step 2: Induction and Deepening

Use your favorite induction and deepening technique to enter a relaxed state.

Step 3: Visualizing the Tranquil Forest

1. **Imagine the Tranquil Forest**: Picture yourself entering a serene and peaceful forest designed to calm your mind and soothe your anxiety and depression. This forest is filled with tall trees, gentle streams, and lush greenery, creating an atmosphere of tranquility and safety. Visualize the sights, sounds, and smells of this place, and let yourself fully immerse yourself in its calming energy.
2. **Describe the Forest**: Think about the details of the forest. Are there specific trees that stand out? Can you hear birds singing or the rustling of leaves? How does it feel to be in this place of deep peace and relaxation?

Step 4: Creating the Peaceful Stream

1. **Imagine a Gentle Stream**: Visualize a clear, flowing stream in the center of your Tranquil Forest. This stream represents calmness, clarity, and the ability to let go of anxious or depressive thoughts. The water flowing from the stream is pure and soothing, symbolizing a clear and peaceful mind.
2. **Describe the Stream**: Think about how your Peaceful Stream looks. Is it surrounded by rocks, flowers, or ferns? How does it make you

feel when you see and hear the water flowing?

Step 5: Using the Peaceful Stream

1. **Visualize Yourself by the Stream**: Picture yourself sitting or lying down comfortably by the stream, feeling completely safe and at ease. See every detail—your posture, your breathing, and your sense of relaxation. Imagine the sound of the stream enhancing your ability to let go of any anxious or depressive thoughts.
2. **Feel the Calm and Peace**: As you listen to the soothing sound of the water, feel a surge of calmness, clarity, and peace. Imagine any worries or negative thoughts dissolving away, replaced by a sense of serenity and relaxation.

Step 6: Embracing Inner Peace

1. **Visualize Inner Peace**: Picture yourself surrounded by the beauty and tranquility of the forest. See yourself breathing deeply, with each breath bringing in peace and each exhale releasing tension. Visualize the sense of inner peace and calm that comes with being in this serene environment.
2. **Feel the Serenity**: Imagine yourself feeling completely relaxed and at peace, with every moment enhancing your sense of well-being and calm. Visualize yourself moving through the forest with ease and contentment, fully immersed in the experience.

Step 7: Positive Suggestions for Calming Anxiety and Depression

While in your Tranquil Forest and near the Peaceful Stream, give yourself some positive suggestions to reinforce your calmness and peace. Repeat these affirmations to yourself:

1. "I am calm and at peace."
2. "I release all worries and negative thoughts."
3. "I am surrounded by tranquility and serenity."

4. "I am in control of my thoughts and emotions."
5. "Each day, I feel more peaceful and relaxed."

Step 8: Returning to Reality

1. **Return from the Visualization**: Imagine gradually returning from your visualization, bringing all the calmness and peace from the exercise with you. See yourself leaving the Tranquil Forest but knowing the benefits stay with you.
2. **Re-enter the Calming Place**: Visualize coming back to your calming place, feeling even more relaxed and at ease.

Step 9: Returning to Wakefulness

When you are ready to end the session, imagine leaving your calming place, feeling refreshed and at peace. Count up from one to five. With each count, feel yourself becoming more alert and ready to engage in your day. By the count of five, open your eyes, feeling refreshed and serene.

Technique: Changing Emotional States Quickly

The Triad, a concept popularized by Tony Robbins, consists of three elements: physiology, focus, and language. By changing these three components, you can effectively shift your emotional state. Here's a technique to help you do just that:

Step 1: Make Yourself Comfortable

Find a quiet, comfortable place where you can sit or stand without being disturbed. Ensure the environment is free of distractions if possible.

Step 2: Physiology – Changing Your Body

1. **Adjust Your Posture**: Stand or sit up straight. Pull your shoulders back and lift your head high. Imagine a string pulling you up from the

top of your head, aligning your spine.

2. **Breathe Deeply**: Take deep, slow breaths. Inhale deeply through your nose, filling your lungs completely, and then exhale slowly through your mouth. Repeat this several times, feeling your body relax with each breath.

3. **Move Your Body**: Shake out any tension. You can stretch your arms above your head, roll your shoulders, or even do a few jumping jacks. Movement helps to energize your body and shift your emotional state.

Step 3: Focus – Directing Your Thoughts

1. **Identify the Current Focus**: Take a moment to recognize what you've been focusing on. If you're feeling down or anxious, you might be fixated on negative thoughts or worries.

2. **Shift Your Focus to Positive Aspects**: Think about something that makes you happy or proud. It could be a recent achievement, a fun memory, or something you're looking forward to. Visualize it clearly in your mind and immerse yourself in the positive feelings it brings.

3. **Gratitude Practice**: Focus on what you're grateful for. List three things you appreciate in your life right now. They can be big or small – the important part is to genuinely feel gratitude for them.

Step 4: Language – Changing Your Self-Talk

1. **Recognize Negative Self-Talk**: Pay attention to the words you've been using in your mind. Are they negative or self-critical?

2. **Replace Negative Words with Positive Ones**: Change the way you talk to yourself. Instead of saying, "I can't handle this," try, "I've got this, and I'll figure it out." Instead of, "I'm so stressed," say, "I'm in control and can manage this."

3. **Use Empowering Statements**: Repeat positive affirmations to yourself. Statements like "I am strong and capable," "I choose to be happy," and "I can handle anything that comes my way" can help

reinforce a positive mindset.

Step 5: Putting It All Together

1. **Combine Physiology, Focus, and Language**: Stand or sit with good posture, breathe deeply, focus on positive aspects of your life, and use empowering language.
2. **Visualize Your Desired State**: Close your eyes and visualize yourself in a positive, confident state. See yourself handling challenges with ease, feeling happy and relaxed, and being the best version of yourself.
3. **Anchor the State**: To help solidify this new state, choose a physical gesture, like squeezing your fist or placing your hand on your heart while visualizing and feeling this positive state. Use this gesture whenever you need to shift your emotional state in the future.

Step 6: Practice Regularly

The more you practice this technique, the more natural it will become. Set aside a few minutes each day to consciously change your physiology, focus, and language. Over time, you'll find it easier to shift your emotional state and maintain a positive outlook.

By changing your physiology, focus, and language, you can effectively manage and shift your emotional state almost immediately. This Triad technique helps you to take control of your emotions and create a more positive, resilient mindset. Practice regularly, and you'll find yourself better equipped to handle life's challenges a lot easier.

Technique: Beach Release Visualization for Letting Go of Negative Thoughts and Stress

Step 1: Make Yourself Comfortable

Find a quiet, comfortable place where you can sit or lie down without being disturbed.

Step 2: Induction and Deepening

Use your favorite induction and deepening technique to enter a relaxed state.

Step 3: Visualizing the Serene Beach

1. **Imagine the Serene Beach**: Picture yourself walking along a beautiful, serene beach designed to help you release negative thoughts and stress. The sand is soft beneath your feet, and the gentle sound of waves lapping at the shore creates a soothing atmosphere. Visualize the sights, sounds, and smells of this place, and let yourself fully immerse in its calming energy.
2. **Describe the Beach**: Think about the details of the beach. Is it surrounded by palm trees, cliffs, or dunes? Can you hear the seagulls or the rustling of palm leaves? How does it feel to be in this peaceful place?

Step 4: Finding the Release Rocks

1. **Imagine Finding Smooth Rocks**: Visualize yourself walking along the beach and finding smooth, flat rocks scattered in the sand. These rocks are perfect for writing your negative thoughts and stressors. Each rock represents a specific worry, fear, or negative thought you want to release.
2. **Describe the Rocks**: Think about how these rocks look and feel. Are they warm from the sun, cool and smooth, or colorful? How does it

make you feel to hold one in your hand?

Step 5: Writing on the Rocks

1. **Visualize Writing Your Thoughts**: Picture yourself picking up a rock and using your finger or a stick to write a negative thought or stressor on its surface. See the words clearly as you write them down. As you write, feel the weight of the thought transferring onto the rock.
2. **Feel the Lightness**: As you write each thought on the rocks, feel a sense of lightness and relief. Imagine the burden lifting from your mind, replaced by a sense of clarity and calm.

Step 6: Releasing the Rocks into the Ocean

1. **Visualize Throwing the Rocks**: Picture yourself standing at the edge of the ocean with the rocks in your hands. One by one, throw each rock into the ocean. Watch as the rocks hit the water and sink beneath the surface, taking your negative thoughts and stressors with them.
2. **Feel the Freedom**: As you throw each rock into the ocean, feel a profound sense of freedom and peace. Imagine all your negative thoughts and stress being carried away by the waves, leaving you feeling light, clear, and at ease.

Step 7: Positive Suggestions for Letting Go

While on your serene beach, having released your negative thoughts and stress into the ocean, give yourself some positive suggestions to reinforce your sense of peace and clarity. Repeat these affirmations to yourself:

1. "I release all negative thoughts and stress."
2. "I am free from worries and fears."
3. "I am calm, clear, and at peace."
4. "I am in control of my thoughts and emotions."
5. "Each day, I feel lighter and more relaxed."

Step 8: Returning to Reality

1. **Return from the Visualization**: Imagine gradually returning from your visualization, bringing all the peace and clarity from the exercise with you. See yourself leaving the serene beach but knowing the benefits stay with you.
2. **Re-enter the Calming Place**: Visualize coming back to your calming place, feeling even more relaxed and at ease.

Step 9: Returning to Wakefulness

When you are ready to end the session, imagine leaving your calming place, feeling refreshed and at peace. Count up from one to five. With each count, feel yourself becoming more alert and ready to engage in your day. By the count of five, open your eyes, feeling refreshed and serene.

Technique: Positive Mindset Garden Visualization

Step 1: Make Yourself Comfortable

Find a quiet, comfortable place where you can sit or lie down without being disturbed.

Step 2: Induction and Deepening

Use your favorite induction and deepening technique to enter a relaxed state.

Step 3: Visualizing the Positive Mindset Garden

1. **Imagine the Positive Mindset Garden**: Picture yourself entering a beautiful, vibrant garden designed to cultivate a positive mindset. This garden is filled with colorful flowers, lush greenery, and the gentle sound of birds singing. Visualize the sights, sounds, and smells of this place, and let yourself fully immerse in its uplifting, calming energy.
2. **Describe the Garden**: Think about the details of your garden. Are there winding pathways, gentle streams, or colorful butterflies? How does it feel to be in this place of positivity and growth?

Step 4: Identifying Positive Thoughts as Flowers

1. **Imagine the Flowers**: Visualize each flower in the garden representing a positive thought or belief. Some flowers may be newly planted, while others are fully bloomed. Each flower is vibrant and beautiful, symbolizing the positive aspects of your mindset that you want to nurture and grow.
2. **Describe the Flowers**: Think about how these flowers look. What colors are they? What type of flowers are they? How do they make you feel when you see them?

Step 5: Watering the Positive Flowers

1. **Visualize Watering the Flowers**: Picture yourself holding a watering can filled with nourishing water. As you walk through the garden, gently water each flower, giving them the care and attention they need to thrive. Imagine the flowers responding by growing stronger and more vibrant.
2. **Feel the Growth and Positivity**: As you water each flower, feel a sense of positivity and growth. Imagine your positive thoughts and beliefs becoming more deeply rooted and flourishing, replacing any doubts or negativity with confidence and joy.

Step 6: Identifying Negative Thoughts as Weeds

1. **Imagine the Weeds**: Visualize any negative thoughts or beliefs in your mind as weeds in the garden. These weeds may be small or large, but they take up space and nutrients that could be used by your positive flowers.
2. **Describe the Weeds**: Think about how these weeds look. Are they thorny, tangled, or dark? How do they make you feel when you see them?

Step 7: Pulling the Weeds

1. **Visualize Removing the Weeds**: Picture yourself walking through the garden and carefully pulling each weed from the soil. As you remove the weeds, imagine yourself letting go of negative thoughts and beliefs, making space for more positive growth.
2. **Feel the Relief and Clarity**: As you pull each weed, feel a sense of relief and clarity. Imagine the garden becoming more beautiful and harmonious, with more space for your positive thoughts to flourish.

Step 8: Positive Suggestions for a Positive Mindset

While in your Positive Mindset Garden, give yourself some positive suggestions to reinforce your positive thoughts and beliefs. Repeat these affirmations to yourself:

1. "I nurture and grow positive thoughts."
2. "I let go of negative thoughts and beliefs."
3. "I am confident, joyful, and at peace."
4. "I focus on the positive aspects of my life."
5. "Each day, my positive mindset grows stronger."

Step 9: Returning to Reality

1. **Return from the Visualization**: Imagine gradually returning from your visualization, bringing all the positivity and clarity from the exercise with you. See yourself leaving the Positive Mindset Garden but knowing the benefits stay with you.
2. **Re-enter the Calming Place**: Visualize coming back to your calming place, feeling even more positive and at ease.

Step 10: Returning to Wakefulness

When you are ready to end the session, imagine leaving your calming place, feeling refreshed and positive. Count up from one to five. With each count, feel yourself becoming more alert and ready to engage in your day. By the count of five, open your eyes, feeling refreshed and positive.

Technique: Mind Control Room Visualization for Managing Mental Health and Thoughts

Step 1: Make Yourself Comfortable

Find a quiet, comfortable place where you can sit or lie down without being disturbed.

Step 2: Induction and Deepening

Use your favorite induction and deepening technique to enter a relaxed state.

Step 3: Visualizing the Mind Control Room

1. **Imagine the Mind Control Room**: Picture yourself entering a high-tech, serene control room designed to give you control over your mental health and thoughts. This room is filled with advanced control panels, screens displaying positive imagery, and comfortable seating. Visualize the sights, sounds, and smells of this place, and let yourself fully immerse in its calming and empowering energy.
2. **Describe the Room**: Think about the details of your control room. Are there touch screens, glowing buttons, or calming ambient lighting? How does it feel to be in this place where you are in complete control?

Step 4: Creating the Control Panels

1. **Imagine the Control Panels**: Visualize several control panels in the room, each representing different aspects of your mental health and thoughts. One panel might control your stress levels, another your positivity, and another your focus and clarity.
2. **Describe the Panels**: Think about how these control panels look. Are they sleek and modern, with various knobs, buttons, and sliders? How does it make you feel to see and use them?

Step 5: Adjusting the Controls

1. **Visualize Adjusting the Controls**: Picture yourself approaching one of the control panels. See yourself adjusting the knobs, buttons, or sliders to fine-tune your mental state. For example, you might turn down the stress level and increase the positivity and focus levels.
2. **Feel the Change**: As you adjust each control, feel a sense of change within you. Imagine your stress melting away, your positivity increasing, and your focus sharpening. Feel yourself becoming more balanced and in control.

Step 6: Monitoring Your Mental State

1. **Visualize Monitoring Your Thoughts**: Picture yourself sitting comfortably in front of a large screen displaying your thoughts. See positive thoughts glowing brightly and negative thoughts as shadows. Visualize yourself using the control panel to transform the negative thoughts into positive ones.
2. **Feel the Control**: As you transform your thoughts, feel a deep sense of control and empowerment. Imagine yourself managing your mental state with ease, knowing you have the tools to maintain balance and positivity.

Step 7: Positive Suggestions for Mental Control

While in your Mind Control Room, give yourself some positive suggestions to reinforce your control over your mental health and thoughts. Repeat these affirmations to yourself:

1. "I am in control of my thoughts and emotions."
2. "I can manage my mental health with ease."
3. "I transform negative thoughts into positive ones."
4. "I am calm, balanced, and empowered."
5. "Each day, I become more in control of my mental state."

Step 8: Returning to Reality

1. **Return from the Visualization**: Imagine gradually returning from your visualization, bringing all the control and empowerment from the exercise with you. See yourself leaving the Mind Control Room but knowing the benefits stay with you.
2. **Re-enter the Calming Place**: Visualize coming back to your calming place, feeling even more in control and at ease.

Step 9: Returning to Wakefulness

When you are ready to end the session, imagine leaving your calming place, feeling refreshed and empowered. Count up from one to five. With each count, feel yourself becoming more alert and ready to engage in your day. By the count of five, open your eyes, feeling refreshed and in control.

<u>Technique: Emotional State Shift</u>

Step 1: Make Yourself Comfortable

Find a quiet, comfortable place where you can sit or lie down without being disturbed.

Step 2: Induction and Deepening

Use your favorite induction and deepening technique to enter a relaxed state.

Step 3: Visualizing the Transformation Garden

1. **Imagine the Transformation Garden**: Picture yourself entering a beautiful, vibrant garden designed to help you transform your emotional state. This garden is filled with colorful flowers, tall trees, and comfortable seating areas. Visualize the sights, sounds, and smells of this place, and let yourself fully immerse in its calming and empowering energy.
2. **Describe the Garden**: Think about the details of your garden. Are there blooming flowers, gentle streams, or inspiring statues? How does it feel to be in this place of peace and transformation?

Step 4: Changing Your Focus

1. **Find the Focus Fountain**: Visualize a serene fountain in your garden. This fountain represents the power of positive focus. Walk towards the fountain and notice how clear and sparkling the water is.
2. **Shift Your Focus**: Imagine dipping your hands into the fountain and feeling the cool, refreshing water. As you do, think about shifting your focus from negative thoughts to positive ones. Let the water symbolize washing away worries and focusing on what brings you joy and satisfaction. Feel the clarity and positivity filling your mind.

Step 5: Changing Your Language

1. **Find the Language Tree**: Visualize a magnificent tree in your garden, full of strong branches and vibrant leaves. This tree represents the power of positive language.
2. **Transform Your Words**: Imagine sitting under the tree and feeling its strength and support. Think about the words you use when talking to yourself. Replace negative phrases with positive, empowering ones. For example, change "I can't" to "I can," and "This is difficult" to "I am capable." Feel the tree's energy reinforcing your new, positive language.

Step 6: Changing Your Physiology

1. **Find the Physiology Pathway**: Visualize a winding pathway in your garden, lined with blooming flowers and lush greenery. This pathway represents the power of positive physical movement.
2. **Enhance Your Physiology**: Imagine walking down the pathway, feeling the earth beneath your feet. As you walk, stand tall, breathe deeply, and move with confidence. Feel your body becoming more energized and powerful with each step. Notice how your physical state influences your emotions, making you feel more uplifted and in control.

Step 7: Embracing the New Emotional State

1. **Visualize Your Transformed Self**: Picture yourself standing in the center of the Transformation Garden, having adjusted your focus, language, and physiology. See yourself radiating positivity, confidence, and empowerment. Visualize how this new emotional state affects your thoughts, actions, and interactions.
2. **Feel the Transformation**: As you embrace your new emotional state, feel a profound sense of well-being and empowerment. Imagine yourself moving through your day with a positive mindset, confident

language, and strong, energized physiology.

Step 8: Positive Suggestions for Maintaining the Transformation

While in your Transformation Garden, give yourself some positive suggestions to reinforce your new emotional state. Repeat these affirmations to yourself:

1. "I focus on the positive aspects of my life."
2. "I use empowering and supportive language."
3. "I maintain a confident and energized physiology."
4. "I am in control of my emotional state."
5. "Each day, I become more positive and empowered."

Step 9: Returning to Reality

1. **Return from the Visualization**: Imagine gradually returning from your visualization, bringing all the positivity and empowerment from the exercise with you. See yourself leaving the Transformation Garden but knowing the benefits stay with you.
2. **Re-enter the Calming Place**: Visualize coming back to your calming place, feeling even more positive and in control of your emotional state.

Step 10: Returning to Wakefulness

When you are ready to end the session, imagine leaving your calming place, feeling refreshed and empowered. Count up from one to five. With each count, feel yourself becoming more alert and ready to engage in your day. By the count of five, open your eyes, feeling refreshed and in control.

Technique: Negative Energy Transformation

Step 1: Make Yourself Comfortable

Find a quiet, comfortable place where you can sit or lie down without being disturbed.

Step 2: Induction and Deepening

Use your favorite induction and deepening technique to enter a relaxed state.

Step 3: Visualizing Negative Energy

1. **Identify the Negative Energy**: Picture yourself becoming aware of any negative energy in your body. This energy might feel like tension, stress, or discomfort. Visualize it as a specific color that represents negativity to you. Perhaps it's a dark or murky color.
2. **Describe the Energy**: Think about how this negative energy looks and feels. Is it swirling, stagnant, or heavy? Where in your body do you feel it the most?

Step 4: Removing the Negative Energy

1. **Visualize Removing the Energy**: Imagine reaching out with your hands and gently pulling the negative energy from your body. See yourself extracting this dark, murky energy, feeling it leave your body and become lighter.
2. **Feel the Lightness**: As you remove the negative energy, feel a sense of relief and lightness. Imagine the areas of your body that held the negative energy becoming clear and free.

Step 5: Spinning the Energy in the Opposite Direction

1. **Visualize Spinning the Energy**: Picture yourself holding the extracted negative energy in front of you. Now, see yourself starting to spin this energy in the opposite direction. As you spin it, notice the energy beginning to change.
2. **Feel the Transformation**: As the energy spins, see it changing color from dark and murky to a bright, peaceful color that represents calm and clarity to you. Maybe it's a soft blue, gentle green, or radiant white. Feel the energy becoming more positive and peaceful with each spin.

Step 6: Reintegrating the Positive Energy

1. **Visualize Reintegrating the Energy**: Once the energy has completely transformed into a color of peace, calm, and clarity, see yourself gently placing this positive energy back into your body. Imagine it flowing into the areas where the negative energy once resided.
2. **Feel the Peace and Calm**: As the positive energy reintegrated into your body, feel a deep sense of peace, calm, and clarity spreading through you. Imagine this peaceful energy filling every part of your being, leaving you feeling refreshed and balanced.

Step 7: Positive Suggestions for Maintaining Positive Energy

While experiencing the positive energy within you, give yourself some positive suggestions to reinforce this new state. Repeat these affirmations to yourself:

1. "I release all negative energy from my body."
2. "I am filled with peace, calm, and clarity."
3. "I am in control of my energy and emotions."
4. "I transform negativity into positivity with ease."
5. "Each day, I feel more balanced and serene."

Step 8: Returning to Reality

1. **Return from the Visualization**: Imagine gradually returning from your visualization, bringing all the positive energy and calmness from the exercise with you. See yourself leaving this transformative state but knowing the benefits stay with you.
2. **Re-enter the Calming Place**: Visualize coming back to your calming place, feeling even more balanced and at ease.

Step 9: Returning to Wakefulness

When you are ready to end the session, imagine leaving your calming place, feeling refreshed and positive. Count up from one to five. With each count, feel yourself becoming more alert and ready to engage in your day. By the count of five, open your eyes, feeling refreshed and balanced.

For additional information on dealing with anxiety or depression, visit https://mindoverthebody.com

If you are dealing with a serious mental health episode, please seek professional help as soon as possible.

Chapter 10: Conquering Fears and Phobias

Spiders, snakes, flying, heights, darkness, and public speaking—these are just a few examples of things, experiences, or thoughts that can evoke intense fears and phobias in people. While it's natural to have fears—they serve a purpose by keeping us safe from potentially dangerous situations—these fears can become problematic when they are based on irrational thoughts or have grown so large that they interfere with our daily lives. When fear starts to hold us back from living fully, it's time to make some changes and move past these phobias.

I'm not suggesting that you'll go from having a panic attack at the sight of a spider to inviting one to crawl on your arm overnight (although I'm not saying that's impossible either). What we're aiming for here is to manage the fear or phobia so it no longer prevents you from doing the things you want or need to do. For instance, if you have an intense fear of flying, you might be missing out on amazing vacations or visits with friends and family. If public speaking terrifies you, it could be holding you back from advancing in your career.

Whatever your fear or phobia is, if it's negatively impacting your life, it's time to change that. And it might be easier than you think.

One of my clients, for example, came to me because he couldn't get into a car without experiencing a major anxiety attack where he felt like he could barely breathe. He had been seeing a psychiatrist for two years without any improvement, so as a last-ditch effort, he scheduled sessions with me. Since he couldn't travel anywhere beyond walking distance, we did our sessions remotely over Zoom.

After our initial conversation, it became clear that the anxiety wasn't the core issue—it was a reaction to his overwhelming fear of being in a car due to an experience years earlier. If we could address and reduce this fear, the anxiety would resolve itself. Using hypnosis, I employed a technique known as dissociation, which involves helping the client see themselves overcoming the fear from an observer's perspective, rather than through their own eyes. This method helps disconnect the intense emotional response, allowing the client to view the fear as irrational and change their reaction to it. Dissociation is one of the most effective ways to alter irrational thoughts or fears.

While I often tell my clients that significant changes can't always be expected in a single session, sometimes it does happen. This was one of those times. When we logged on for our second session, I asked how his week had been and if he had noticed any changes. He laughed and told me that after our first session, he went out for a drive and experienced zero issues. He even saw new buildings around town that hadn't been built the last time he was out. Immediate change can happen; the key is to keep going even if it doesn't happen right away.

The reason his psychiatrist wasn't able to help him over two years while I could assist him in under an hour is simple: we were working on different areas of the mind. The psychiatrist was trying to rationalize the fear by discussing it at the conscious level, but the fear didn't live there. Once we tapped into the subconscious mind, the change was fast, easy, and permanent.

The self-hypnosis techniques I'm about to share are designed to help you dissociate from your fear, to disconnect the emotional response. However, if you feel that your fear or phobia is too intense to handle on your own, working with a professional trained and experienced in dealing with fears and phobias can be incredibly helpful. They can guide you through the process, helping to disconnect the emotional response and manage any abreactions that might arise.

Fears and phobias can be managed and even overcome through hypnosis and self-hypnosis techniques, in fact, it's probably the most effective way to overcome them. By addressing the root cause and altering the subconscious response, you can reclaim control over your life and stop letting these fears hold you back. With practice and the right approach, moving past these fears is not only possible but can be quicker and easier than you ever imagined.

Technique: Overcoming Fears and Phobias Movie Theater

Step 1: Make Yourself Comfortable

Find a quiet, comfortable place where you can sit or lie down without being disturbed. Ensure the environment is free of distractions.

Step 2: Induction and Deepening

Use your favorite induction and deepening technique to enter a relaxed state.

Step 3: Visualizing the Movie Theater

1. **Imagine the Movie Theater**: Picture yourself entering a comfortable, private movie theater. This theater is a safe and controlled environment where you can observe your fears and phobias from a distance. Visualize the sights, sounds, and smells of this place, and let yourself fully immerse in its calm and secure atmosphere.
2. **Describe the Theater**: Think about the details of the theater. Are there plush seats, a large screen, and soft lighting? How does it feel to be in this place of safety and control?

Step 4: Watching Yourself on the Screen

1. **Imagine the Movie Screen**: Visualize a large movie screen in front of you. This screen will show a movie of yourself experiencing the fear or phobia, but you will be watching it as an observer, dissociated from the scene itself.
2. **Describe the Scene**: Think about how the scene looks. Is it clear and vivid, or slightly hazy? What is happening in the scene? How does it feel to watch yourself from a distance?

Step 5: Watching the Movie

1. **Visualize Watching the Movie**: Picture yourself sitting comfortably in the theater, watching the movie yourself experiencing the fear or phobia. See every detail—your actions, your expressions, and the environment. As you watch, remind yourself that you are safe and in control, observing from a distance.
2. **Feel the Dissociation**: As you watch the movie, feel a sense of detachment and dissociation from the scene. You are simply an observer, watching yourself from a safe and secure place.

Step 6: Changing the Scene

1. **Visualize Changing the Movie**: Imagine you have a remote control that allows you to change the movie. Use the remote to gradually change the scene, making it less intense and more manageable. For example, you might turn down the volume, slow down the action, or change the colors to black and white.
2. **Feel the Control**: As you make these changes, feel a sense of control and empowerment. You are in charge of the movie, and you can make it as comfortable and manageable as you need.

Step 7: Transforming the Fear

1. **Visualize a Positive Outcome**: Once you have made the scene more manageable, visualize a positive outcome. See yourself overcoming the fear or phobia with confidence and ease. Imagine the scene ending with you feeling calm, empowered, and in control.
2. **Feel the Success**: As you visualize the positive outcome, feel a sense of success and empowerment. Imagine yourself moving through your fear with confidence and ease, fully in control of the situation.

Step 8: Positive Suggestions for Overcoming Fear

While in your movie theater, give yourself some positive suggestions to reinforce your ability to overcome fear and phobias. Repeat these affirmations to yourself:

1. "I am in control of my fears and phobias."
2. "I observe my fears from a safe and detached place."
3. "I can change and manage my fear response."
4. "I am confident and empowered in any situation."
5. "Each day, I become stronger and more resilient."

Step 9: Returning to Reality

1. **Return from the Visualization**: Imagine gradually returning from your visualization, bringing all the empowerment and control from the exercise with you. See yourself leaving the movie theater but knowing the benefits stay with you.
2. **Re-enter the Calming Place**: Visualize coming back to your calming place, feeling even more in control and at ease.

Step 10: Returning to Wakefulness

When you are ready to end the session, imagine leaving your calming place, feeling refreshed and empowered. Count up from one to five. With each count, feel yourself becoming more alert and ready to engage in your day. By the count of five, open your eyes, feeling refreshed and in control.

Technique: Overcoming Fears and Phobias with the Balloon Release Visualization

Step 1: Make Yourself Comfortable

Find a quiet, comfortable place where you can sit or lie down without being disturbed. Ensure the environment is free of distractions.

Step 2: Induction and Deepening

Use your favorite induction and deepening technique to enter a relaxed state.

Step 3: Visualizing the Tranquil Meadow

1. **Imagine the Tranquil Meadow**: Picture yourself entering a beautiful, serene meadow designed to help you overcome your fears and phobias. This meadow is filled with colorful flowers, soft grass, and gentle breezes. Visualize the sights, sounds, and smells of this place, and let yourself fully immerse in its calming energy.
2. **Describe the Meadow**: Think about the details of the meadow. Are there birds singing, butterflies fluttering, or a gentle stream flowing nearby? How does it feel to be in this place of peace and tranquility?

Step 4: Identifying Your Fears and Phobias

1. **Visualize Your Fears as Balloons**: Imagine that each fear or phobia you have is represented by a balloon. These balloons may be different colors, sizes, or shapes, each symbolizing a specific fear or phobia.
2. **Describe the Balloons**: Think about how these balloons look. Are some of them large and dark, while others are smaller and lighter? How does it feel to see these balloons representing your fears?

Step 5: Releasing the Balloons

1. **Visualize Holding the Balloons**: Picture yourself holding all the balloons representing your fears and phobias. Feel the weight of them in your hands, and recognize the power they have over you.
2. **Feel the Lightness**: As you hold the balloons, take a deep breath and prepare to let them go. Feel a sense of anticipation and readiness to release these fears.

Step 6: Letting Go of the Balloons

1. **Visualize Releasing the Balloons**: Imagine yourself standing in the middle of the tranquil meadow, holding the balloons. One by one, release each balloon into the sky. Watch as they float higher and higher, becoming smaller and smaller until they disappear completely.
2. **Feel the Freedom**: As you release each balloon, feel a profound sense of freedom and relief. Imagine all your fears and phobias drifting away, leaving you feeling lighter, calmer, and more in control.

Step 7: Transforming the Negative Energy

1. **Visualize the Balloons Transforming**: As the balloons float away, imagine them transforming into bright, positive colors, symbolizing peace, calm, and clarity. See the sky filled with beautiful, colorful balloons representing your newfound strength and resilience.
2. **Feel the Transformation**: As you watch the transformation, feel a deep sense of empowerment and confidence. Know that you have the ability to overcome your fears and phobias and that they no longer have control over you.

Step 8: Positive Suggestions for Overcoming Fear

While in your Tranquil Meadow, give yourself some positive suggestions to reinforce your ability to overcome fear and phobias. Repeat these affirmations to yourself:

1. "I release all fears and phobias."
2. "I am in control of my thoughts and emotions."
3. "I am calm, confident, and at peace."
4. "I transform fear into strength and resilience."
5. "Each day, I become stronger and more empowered."

Step 9: Returning to Reality

1. **Return from the Visualization**: Imagine gradually returning from your visualization, bringing all the empowerment and peace from the exercise with you. See yourself leaving the Tranquil Meadow but knowing the benefits stay with you.
2. **Re-enter the Calming Place**: Visualize coming back to your calming place, feeling even more in control and at ease.

Step 10: Returning to Wakefulness

When you are ready to end the session, imagine leaving your calming place, feeling refreshed and empowered. Count up from one to five. With each count, feel yourself becoming more alert and ready to engage in your day. By the count of five, open your eyes, feeling refreshed and in control.

Technique: Overcoming the Fear of Public Speaking with the Stage Visualization

Step 1: Make Yourself Comfortable

Find a quiet, comfortable place where you can sit or lie down without being disturbed. Ensure the environment is free of distractions.

Step 2: Induction and Deepening

Use your favorite induction and deepening technique to enter a relaxed state.

Step 3: Visualizing the Safe Theater

1. **Imagine the Safe Theater**: Picture yourself entering a beautiful, serene theater designed to help you overcome your fear of public speaking. This theater is cozy and inviting, with plush seats, soft lighting, and a calm atmosphere. Visualize the sights, sounds, and smells of this place, and let yourself fully immerse in its calming energy.
2. **Describe the Theater**: Think about the details of the theater. Are there gentle spotlights, velvet curtains, or a soothing background hum? How does it feel to be in this place of peace and security?

Step 4: Visualizing the Stage

1. **Imagine the Stage**: Visualize a stage in the theater, well-lit and welcoming. See yourself standing confidently on this stage, ready to speak to an audience. Picture the stage as a place of power and potential, where you can express yourself freely and confidently.
2. **Describe the Stage**: Think about the details of the stage. Is it large or small, decorated simply or elaborately? How does it feel to stand on this stage, knowing you are in control?

Step 5: Observing Yourself from the Audience

1. **Visualize Watching Yourself**: Imagine sitting in the audience, watching yourself on the stage. See yourself speaking confidently, engaging with the audience, and delivering your message clearly. You are an observer, watching yourself perform successfully.
2. **Feel the Detachment**: As you watch yourself from the audience, feel a sense of detachment and calm. You are safe and in control, observing from a distance.

Step 6: Transforming the Fear

1. **Visualize Transforming the Scene**: Imagine you have a remote control that allows you to change the scene on stage. Use the remote to enhance your confidence, clarity, and presence. Turn up the brightness, increase the volume of your voice, and see yourself standing taller and more self-assured.
2. **Feel the Confidence**: As you make these changes, feel a sense of confidence and empowerment growing within you. See yourself speaking with ease and poise, fully in control of your emotions and the situation.

Step 7: Rehearsing the Positive Outcome

1. **Visualize the Positive Outcome**: Picture yourself delivering your speech flawlessly. The audience is engaged, nodding, and responding positively. You feel calm, confident, and successful. Visualize the scene ending with applause and a sense of accomplishment.
2. **Feel the Success**: As you rehearse the positive outcome, feel a deep sense of success and empowerment. Imagine yourself moving through your speech with confidence and ease, knowing you can handle any situation.

Step 8: Positive Suggestions for Public Speaking

While in your Safe Theater, give yourself some positive suggestions to reinforce your ability to overcome the fear of public speaking. Repeat these affirmations to yourself:

1. "I am confident and calm when speaking in public."
2. "I engage with my audience easily and effectively."
3. "I deliver my message clearly and confidently."
4. "I am in control of my thoughts and emotions while speaking."
5. "Each time I speak, I become more confident and successful."

Step 9: Returning to Reality

1. **Return from the Visualization**: Imagine gradually returning from your visualization, bringing all the confidence and calmness from the exercise with you. See yourself leaving the Safe Theater but knowing the benefits stay with you.
2. **Re-enter the Calming Place**: Visualize coming back to your calming place, feeling even more in control and at ease.

Step 10: Returning to Wakefulness

When you are ready to end the session, imagine leaving your calming place, feeling refreshed and empowered. Count up from one to five. With each count, feel yourself becoming more alert and ready to engage in your day. By the count of five, open your eyes, feeling refreshed and in control.

By incorporating these self-hypnosis techniques into your routine, you can conquer your fears and phobias and build confidence in challenging situations.

Chapter 11: Weight Loss and Healthy Habits

Tired of yo-yo dieting, fad diets that are unsustainable, The latest supplement or medication, or starving yourself to death? Good, then let's drop some pounds the easier, more sustainable way. Changing your relationship with food.

Hypnosis isn't a magic wand that melts fat. Too many people think that if they use hypnosis they can just keep doing and eating the same way and the hypnosis will take care of burning fat. Hypnosis in weight loss is about getting you to make shifts in the way you eat, about creating new habits and beliefs.

Now my hypno-diet plan is pretty simple. There are only a few rules:

Eat what you want and like.

For any diet to be sustainable, you have to eat what you like. The key is eating less of it. While our goal is to get you to enjoy eating healthier, the reality is that weight loss has very little to do with what you eat. You can lose weight eating nothing but Twinkies, although that wouldn't be the healthiest choice....

Eat when you're hungry.

Starving yourself is actually slowing down your metabolism. We were never designed to eat 2 or 3 meals a day.

Check-in with your stomach between each bite.

The communication between the stomach and mind is slow.... It can take 10-15 minutes for the "Full" signal to be received and processed, so by the time we get that signal we may have already gobbled up our heaping, supersized, unhealthy meal. By checking in with the stomach between bites, we can stop eating when we are comfortably at a 6 on a scale of 0-10 (0 being "I'm so hungry that I'm going to eat my own arm and 10 being food coma territory)

Put the fork, spoon, or food down between bites.

PERSONAL TRANSFORMATION FROM WITHIN: THE POWER OF SELF HYPNOSIS FOR LASTING CHANGE

Mindless eating is one of the biggest reasons we are such an overweight society these days. We get so distracted by our computers, phones, and television that we are loading up the next bite before we have even chewed the one in our mouth. Let's face it, most people only chew enough to not choke. So on this plan, you are going to pay attention, chew your food, and put the fork, spoon, or food down while you do it.

Now to bring this all together and start "wanting" to eat healthier, and eat less, we bring in hypnosis to let our subconscious in on our plan of action. Normally when I work with someone for weight loss it is a four-session commitment, but often those clients have a substantial amount of weight to lose and want to lose it as quickly as possible for health reasons. In those cases, I use a hypno-gastric bypass technique to reduce the amount the stomach thinks that it can even hold. To find out more about losing substantial weight quickly you can go to my website at mindoverthebody.com, but regardless of the amount of weight you want to lose, this method is a solid foundation to build on.

For normal weight loss goals, the techniques that I'm going to lay out for you will get the scale moving in the right direction as long as it's really what YOU want. Remember, it has to be for you, not because someone else is telling you to lose weight. If your doctor says you need to lose weight, ignore them, if your husband, wife, boyfriend, or girlfriend is telling you that you need to lose weight, get a new one. This has to be for you, and what you truly want.

The first thing we have to discuss is that weight loss is a slow process and it's going to take commitment. You can't expect one hypnosis or self-hypnosis session to just all of the sudden make you eat less, eat healthier, want to exercise, not want to buy a gallon of double fudge cookie dough ice cream, or eat a bag of chips in one sitting. Weight loss is a commitment, but it doesn't have to be hard or unsatisfying. It can be an easy process.

Before we move on to the methods, let's go over a few optional items on this plan.

1. You don't have to count your daily calories, but for me, I actually get some satisfaction from counting them. When I realize that I can be completely satisfied throughout the day by eating 800 calories less than I used to, it gives me more motivation and proves to the mind

that we don't need as much food as we used to think we needed, or wanted.

2. If you are going to weigh yourself, do it every day at the same time and only care about the weekly average. If you get hung up on a one or two-day increase in weight it is going to make you think that it's not working. The reality is that any change that we make in our eating habits can lead to some water weight gain. Also just because we ate less and exercised doesn't mean that we are going to see an immediate drop in the scale, you might not see a change for 2-3 days.

3. Remember it takes a cumulative deficit of 3500 calories to lose a pound of fat. Do what you can in the form of increased physical activity to help burn those calories and create the deficit.

4. When you are in the bathroom in the morning getting ready to start your day, look in a full-length mirror if you have one and say out loud, "Hello Beautiful" or "Hello Handsome". Your body didn't cause the issue with the extra weight, your mind did. It's time to appreciate our body in whatever condition it's currently in and start showing it some love instead of walking past the mirror and feeling disgusted, ashamed, or disappointed. Now say "I'm sorry for the way I treated you in the past, but I'm committed to changing that now."

Let's start with creating the physical body we want and trying it on for size.

Technique: The Ideal Body Mirror

Step 1: Make Yourself Comfortable

Find a quiet, comfortable place where you can sit or lie down without being disturbed. Ensure the environment is free of distractions.

Step 2: Induction and Deepening

Use your favorite induction and deepening technique to enter a relaxed state.

Step 3: Entering the Visualization

1. **Imagine the Ideal Body Mirror**: Picture yourself in a comfortable room with a large, full-length mirror in front of you. This mirror is magical, allowing you to create the reflection of your ideal body. Visualize the sights, sounds, and feelings of this place, and let yourself fully immerse in its positive and motivating energy.
2. **Describe the Mirror**: Think about the details of the mirror. Is it framed in gold or silver? Is the glass clear and bright? How does it feel to be in this place where you can visualize your ideal self?

Step 4: Creating Your Ideal Body

1. **Visualize Your Ideal Body**: Look into the mirror and see the reflection of your ideal body. Notice the details of this ideal version of yourself—your shape, posture, and overall appearance. Imagine the confidence and happiness radiating from this reflection. Make sure it is exactly the way you want it.
2. **Describe Your Ideal Body**: Think about how your ideal body looks and feels. What changes do you notice in your reflection? How does it feel to see this version of yourself?

Step 5: Stepping into the Mirror

1. **Visualize Stepping into the Mirror**: Imagine yourself stepping into the mirror and merging with your ideal body. Feel yourself becoming one with this ideal version of yourself. Notice how it feels in this body—feel the way it feels. Make sure it is exactly the right ideal body, if not, make changes now.
2. **Feel the Transformation**: As you step into the mirror, feel a sense of transformation. Imagine your body adjusting to this new, ideal shape and size. Feel the confidence and motivation of being in your ideal body.

Step 6: Positive Suggestions for Weight Loss

While inhabiting your ideal body and practicing mindful eating, give yourself some positive suggestions to reinforce your commitment to weight loss and healthy habits. Repeat these affirmations to yourself:

1. "I am in control of my eating habits."
2. "I listen to my body and stop eating when I am satisfied."
3. "I am committed to achieving and maintaining my ideal body."
4. "I make healthy choices that support my weight loss goals."
5. "Each day, I move closer to my healthiest and happiest self."

Step 7: Returning to Reality

1. **Return from the Visualization**: Imagine gradually returning from your visualization, bringing all the confidence and motivation from the exercise with you. See yourself stepping out of the mirror but knowing the benefits stay with you.
2. **Re-enter the Calming Place**: Visualize coming back to your calming place, feeling even more determined and ready to take action towards your weight loss goals.

Step 8: Returning to Wakefulness

When you are ready to end the session, imagine leaving your calming place, feeling refreshed and empowered. Count up from one to five. With each count, feel yourself becoming more alert and ready to engage in your day. By the count of five, open your eyes, feeling refreshed and in control.

Technique: Mindful Eating Visualization for Weight Loss

Step 1: Make Yourself Comfortable

Find a quiet, comfortable place where you can sit or lie down without being disturbed. Ensure the environment is free of distractions.

Step 2: Induction and Deepening

Use your favorite induction and deepening technique to enter a relaxed state.

Step 3: Entering the Visualization

1. **Imagine a Peaceful Dining Setting**: Picture yourself in a dining area. This could be a place where you enjoy eating or one you create in your imagination. This place is beautifully set up with a comfortable chair, a nicely arranged table, and calming surroundings. Visualize the sights, sounds, and feelings of this place, and let yourself fully immerse in its peaceful and relaxing energy.
2. **Describe the Setting**: Think about the details of the dining area. Are there candles, soft lighting, or gentle music playing in the background? How does it feel to be in this place where you can enjoy your meal mindfully?

Step 4: Practicing Mindful Eating

1. **Visualize Mindful Eating Habits**: Picture yourself sitting down to a meal in this setting. Imagine taking your time to fully enjoy each bite of food. Visualize yourself checking in with your stomach after each bite, assessing your hunger level on a scale from 0 to 10, with 0 being empty and 10 being overstuffed.
2. **Chewing Fully**: See yourself chewing each bite thoroughly, savoring the flavors and textures of the food. Feel the pleasure of eating

mindfully and the satisfaction it brings.

3. **Putting Down Utensils**: Visualize yourself putting down your fork, spoon, or food between each bite. Imagine taking a moment to breathe and check in with your stomach before picking up your utensils again.

4. **Stopping at a 6**: Aim to stop eating when you reach a 6 on the hunger-fullness scale, which represents feeling satisfied but not overly full. Visualize yourself recognizing this point and comfortably stopping eating.

Step 5: Visualizing the Benefits

1. **Visualize the Benefits of Mindful Eating**: Picture the positive changes that come from practicing mindful eating—feeling more satisfied with less food, having more energy, and experiencing better digestion. Visualize yourself enjoying these benefits and feeling healthier and more in control.

2. **Feel the Empowerment**: As you visualize these benefits, feel a sense of empowerment and confidence. Know that you have the ability to maintain these healthy eating habits.

Step 6: Positive Suggestions for Mindful Eating

While practicing mindful eating, give yourself some positive suggestions to reinforce your commitment to healthy eating habits. Repeat these affirmations to yourself:

1. "I check in with my stomach after each bite."
2. "I chew my food thoroughly and enjoy each bite."
3. "I put down my utensils between bites to savor my food."
4. "I stop eating when I am satisfied at a level 6."
5. "I am in control of my eating habits and choose to eat mindfully."

Step 7: Embracing the Benefits

1. **Visualize the Benefits of Mindful Eating**: Picture the positive changes that come from practicing mindful eating—feeling more satisfied with less food, having more energy, and experiencing better digestion. Visualize yourself enjoying these benefits and feeling healthier and more in control.
2. **Feel the Empowerment**: As you visualize these benefits, feel a sense of empowerment and confidence. Know that you have the ability to maintain these healthy eating habits.

Step 8: Returning to Reality

1. **Return from the Visualization**: Imagine gradually returning from your visualization, bringing all the mindfulness and control from the exercise with you. See yourself leaving the serene dining area but knowing the benefits stay with you.
2. **Re-enter the Calming Place**: Visualize coming back to your calming place, feeling even more determined and ready to practice mindful eating.

Step 9: Returning to Wakefulness

When you are ready to end the session, imagine leaving your calming place, feeling refreshed and empowered. Count up from one to five. With each count, feel yourself becoming more alert and ready to engage in your day. By the count of five, open your eyes, feeling refreshed and in control.

Technique: Creating Healthy Cravings

Step 1: Make Yourself Comfortable

Find a quiet, comfortable place where you can sit or lie down without being disturbed. Ensure the environment is free of distractions.

Step 2: Induction and Deepening

Use your favorite induction and deepening technique to enter a relaxed state.

Step 3: Entering the Visualization

1. **Imagine a Kitchen**: Picture yourself in a beautifully designed kitchen. This kitchen is filled with natural light, calm colors, and a peaceful atmosphere. Visualize the sights, sounds, and feelings of this place, and let yourself fully immerse in its calming and positive energy.
2. **Describe the Kitchen**: Think about the details of the kitchen. Are there large windows, a wooden dining table, or fresh herbs on the windowsill? How does it feel to be in this place of calm and inspiration?

Step 4: Seeing the Two Options

1. **Visualize Two Plates**: Imagine two plates in front of you on the kitchen counter. One plate is filled with unhealthy, high-calorie foods and snacks, while the other is filled with fresh, nutritious, and healthy food options. Take a moment to observe each plate.
2. **Describe the Plates**: Think about how the foods on each plate look. Are the unhealthy foods greasy, sugary, or processed? Are the healthy foods colorful, fresh, and appetizing?

Step 5: Feeling the Attraction to Healthy Foods

1. **Visualize the Healthy Foods**: Focus your attention on the plate with healthy foods. Imagine the vibrant colors, fresh smells, and appealing textures. Feel a growing sense of attraction and craving for these healthy options.
2. **Feel the Desire**: As you visualize healthy foods, feel a strong desire to choose and eat them. Imagine your body naturally craving the nutrients and energy that these healthy foods provide.

Step 6: Choosing Healthy Foods

1. **Visualize Choosing the Healthy Plate**: Picture yourself reaching out and picking up the plate with healthy foods. Feel the excitement and satisfaction of making a positive choice for your health.
2. **Feel the Commitment**: As you choose a healthy plate, feel a deep sense of commitment to nourishing your body with the best possible foods. Imagine yourself feeling proud and motivated by your decision.

Step 7: Enjoying Healthy Foods

1. **Visualize Eating Healthy Foods**: Imagine yourself sitting down at the kitchen table and enjoying the healthy foods on your plate. Savor each bite, appreciating the flavors, textures, and nourishing benefits of the food. Feel the satisfaction and energy that comes from eating well.
2. **Feel the Satisfaction**: As you enjoy healthy foods, feel a sense of contentment and well-being. Imagine how choosing healthy foods positively impacts your body and mind.

Step 8: Positive Suggestions for Healthy Food Choices

While visualizing these healthy food choices and meals, give yourself some positive suggestions to reinforce your commitment to a healthy diet. Repeat these affirmations to yourself:

1. "I crave healthy, nutritious foods."
2. "I choose foods that nourish and energize my body."
3. "I enjoy preparing and eating healthy meals."
4. "I feel proud and motivated by my healthy food choices."
5. "Each day, I make decisions that support my health and well-being."
6. "I easily avoid unhealthy high-calorie foods and snacks."
7. "I am in control of my cravings and choose healthy options."

Step 9: Embracing the Benefits

1. **Visualize the Benefits of Healthy Eating**: Picture the positive changes that come from making healthier food choices—feeling more energetic, improving your overall health, and experiencing greater well-being. Visualize yourself enjoying these benefits and feeling healthier and more in control.
2. **Feel the Empowerment**: As you visualize these benefits, feel a sense of empowerment and confidence. Know that you have the ability to maintain these healthy eating habits.

Step 10: Returning to Reality

1. **Return from the Visualization**: Imagine gradually returning from your visualization, bringing all the mindfulness and control from the exercise with you. See yourself leaving the tranquil kitchen but knowing the benefits stay with you.
2. **Re-enter the Calming Place**: Visualize coming back to your calming place, feeling even more determined and ready to make healthier food choices.

Step 11: Returning to Wakefulness

When you are ready to end the session, imagine leaving your calming place, feeling refreshed and empowered. Count up from one to five. With each count, feel yourself becoming more alert and ready to engage in your day. By the count of five, open your eyes, feeling refreshed and in control.

Technique: Creating a Desire to Exercise

Step 1: Make Yourself Comfortable

Find a quiet, comfortable place where you can sit or lie down without being disturbed. Ensure the environment is free of distractions.

Step 2: Induction and Deepening

Use your favorite induction and deepening technique to enter a relaxed state.
Step 3: Entering the Visualization

1. **Imagine a Motivating Fitness Space**: Picture yourself in a fitness space. This could be a gym, an outdoor park, or any place where you might feel motivated to exercise. Visualize the sights, sounds, and feelings of this place.
2. **Describe the Space**: Think about the details of the fitness space. Are there vibrant colors, people working out, and upbeat music playing? How does it feel to be in this place of energy and motivation?

Step 4: Visualizing Your Ideal Workout

1. **Visualize Your Exercise Routine**: Imagine yourself engaging in a workout that you enjoy and that aligns with your weight loss goals. This could be running, cycling, weight lifting, yoga, walking, or any other form of exercise. See yourself moving with ease and strength.
2. **Feel the Enjoyment**: As you visualize your workout, feel a growing sense of enjoyment and satisfaction. Imagine yourself loving the movement, the rhythm, and the effort. Feel the endorphins that come from exercising.

Step 5: Setting Exercise Goals

1. **Visualize Your Goals**: Picture a board or a screen in your fitness

space where you can write down your exercise goals. These goals might include the number of workouts per week, specific activities, or fitness milestones you want to achieve.

2. **Feel the Commitment**: As you write down your goals, feel a deep sense of commitment and determination. Imagine yourself feeling excited and motivated to achieve these goals.

Step 6: Overcoming Barriers

1. **Visualize Removing Obstacles**: Imagine any barriers or excuses that have kept you from exercising as small rocks or weights. Visualize yourself lifting and moving these obstacles out of your path, clearing the way for your fitness journey.

2. **Feel the Empowerment**: As you remove each obstacle, feel a sense of empowerment and control. Know that you have the ability to overcome any barriers to your exercise routine.

Step 7: Embracing the Benefits

1. **Visualize the Benefits of Exercise**: Picture the positive changes that come from regular exercise—feeling more energetic, losing weight, improving your overall health, and experiencing greater well-being. Visualize yourself enjoying these benefits and feeling healthier and more in control.

2. **Feel the Motivation**: As you visualize these benefits, feel a strong sense of motivation and desire to exercise regularly. Know that each workout brings you closer to your weight loss goals and overall health.

Step 8: Positive Suggestions for Exercise

While visualizing your workout and the benefits of exercise, give yourself some positive suggestions to reinforce your commitment to a regular fitness routine. Repeat these affirmations to yourself:

1. "I enjoy exercising and look forward to my workouts."
2. "Exercise is a rewarding and essential part of my life."
3. "I am motivated and committed to achieving my fitness goals."
4. "Each workout brings me closer to my weight loss goals."
5. "I am strong, energetic, and love taking care of my body."

Step 9: Returning to Reality

1. **Return from the Visualization**: Imagine gradually returning from your visualization, bringing all the motivation and energy from the exercise with you. See yourself leaving the motivating fitness space but knowing the benefits stay with you.
2. **Re-enter the Calming Place**: Visualize coming back to your calming place, feeling even more determined and ready to incorporate regular exercise into your routine.

Step 10: Returning to Wakefulness

When you are ready to end the session, imagine leaving your calming place, feeling refreshed and empowered. Count up from one to five. With each count, feel yourself becoming more alert and ready to engage in your day. By the count of five, open your eyes, feeling refreshed and in control.

Technique: Staying Motivated to Lose Weight

Step 1: Make Yourself Comfortable

Find a quiet, comfortable place where you can sit or lie down without being disturbed. Ensure the environment is free of distractions.

Step 2: Induction and Deepening

Use your favorite induction and deepening technique to enter a relaxed state.

Step 3: Entering the Visualization

1. **Imagine a Path to Your Goal**: Picture yourself standing at the beginning of a beautiful, well-defined path. This path represents your weight loss journey. Visualize the sights, sounds, and feelings of this place.
2. **Describe the Path**: Think about the details of the path. Is it lined with trees, flowers, or motivational signs? How does it feel to be on this path to success?

Step 4: Visualizing Your Goals

1. **Visualize Your Weight Loss Goals**: Imagine seeing your weight loss goals clearly marked along the path. These goals could be specific milestones, such as losing a certain number of pounds, fitting into a favorite outfit, or achieving a fitness goal. See these goals as vibrant markers along the way.
2. **Feel the Excitement**: As you visualize each goal, feel a sense of excitement and anticipation. Imagine the joy and pride you will feel as you reach each milestone.

Step 5: Overcoming Challenges

1. **Visualize Obstacles and Solutions**: Picture any challenges or

obstacles you might face on your weight loss journey as small hurdles or rocks on the path. See yourself easily overcoming these obstacles with creative solutions and determination.

2. **Feel the Empowerment**: As you overcome each challenge, feel a sense of empowerment and resilience. Know that you have the strength and resourcefulness to navigate any difficulties.

Step 6: Embracing Positive Changes

1. **Visualize Positive Lifestyle Changes**: Imagine yourself adopting healthy habits that support your weight loss journey. See yourself enjoying nutritious meals, engaging in regular exercise, staying hydrated, and getting enough sleep. Visualize these habits becoming a natural and enjoyable part of your daily routine.
2. **Feel the Benefits**: As you embrace these positive changes, feel a sense of well-being and vitality. Imagine how these habits enhance your life and contribute to your weight loss success.

Step 7: Maintaining Motivation

1. **Visualize a Source of Motivation**: Picture a motivational source at the end of the path, such as a loved one cheering you on, a personal achievement award, or a vision of your healthiest self. See this source radiating positive energy and encouragement.
2. **Feel the Motivation**: As you focus on this source of motivation, feel a strong sense of determination and drive. Imagine this energy fueling your commitment to your weight loss journey.

Step 8: Positive Suggestions for Staying Motivated

While visualizing your weight loss journey and sources of motivation, give yourself some positive suggestions to reinforce your commitment. Repeat these affirmations to yourself:

1. "I am committed to achieving my weight loss goals."

2. "Every step I take brings me closer to my ideal weight."
3. "I enjoy making healthy choices that support my weight loss."
4. "I overcome challenges with confidence and resilience."
5. "I stay motivated and focused on my weight loss journey."

Step 9: Returning to Reality

1. **Return from the Visualization**: Imagine gradually returning from your visualization, bringing all the motivation and positivity from the exercise with you. See yourself leaving the path to success but knowing the benefits stay with you.
2. **Re-enter the Calming Place**: Visualize coming back to your calming place, feeling even more determined and ready to stay committed to your weight loss journey.

Step 10: Returning to Wakefulness

When you are ready to end the session, imagine leaving your calming place, feeling refreshed and empowered. Count up from one to five. With each count, feel yourself becoming more alert and ready to engage in your day. By the count of five, open your eyes, feeling refreshed and in control.

Technique: Overcoming Cravings for Unhealthy Foods

Step 1: Make Yourself Comfortable

Find a quiet, comfortable place where you can sit or lie down without being disturbed. Ensure the environment is free of distractions.

Step 2: Induction and Deepening

Use your favorite induction and deepening technique to enter a relaxed state.

Step 3: Entering the Visualization

1. **Imagine a Beautiful Garden**: Picture yourself in a beautiful, tranquil garden. This garden is filled with vibrant flowers, lush greenery, and a calming atmosphere. Visualize the sights, sounds, and feelings of this place, and let yourself fully immerse in its peaceful and rejuvenating energy.
2. **Describe the Garden**: Think about the details of the garden. Are there pathways, a fountain, or benches? How does it feel to be in this place of tranquility and beauty?

Step 4: Identifying the Cravings

1. **Visualize the Cravings as Weeds**: Imagine that your cravings for unhealthy foods are like weeds growing in your beautiful garden. These weeds are taking up space and energy that could be used for growing healthy, nourishing plants.
2. **Describe the Weeds**: Think about how these weeds look and feel. Are they large and tangled, or small and persistent? How does it feel to see them in your garden?

Step 5: Removing the Weeds

1. **Visualize Pulling Out the Weeds**: Imagine yourself walking through the garden and gently pulling out each weed by its roots. As you remove each weed, say to yourself, "I release my craving for _________________ and choose health and nourishment."

○ For example, "I release my craving for sugary snacks and choose health and nourishment."

2. **Feel the Release**: As you remove each weed, feel a sense of release and relief. Imagine the space and energy being freed up for healthy, positive growth.

Step 6: Planting Healthy Seeds

1. **Visualize Planting Healthy Seeds**: After removing the weeds, imagine planting healthy seeds in their place. These seeds represent your new, healthy habits and choices. Visualize yourself planting them and imagine them growing strong and healthy.
2. **Feel the Growth**: As you plant these seeds, feel a sense of hope and possibility. Imagine these new habits taking root and flourishing, symbolizing your commitment to a healthier lifestyle.

Step 7: Nurturing the Garden

1. **Visualize Caring for the Garden**: Spend a few moments nurturing your garden. Imagine watering the new seeds, providing sunlight, and caring for the existing plants. This represents nurturing your healthy habits and choices.
2. **Feel the Satisfaction**: As you care for your garden, feel a sense of satisfaction and accomplishment. Visualize the garden flourishing, symbolizing your growing strength and determination to overcome cravings.

Step 8: Positive Suggestions for Overcoming Cravings

While in your beautiful garden, give yourself some positive suggestions to reinforce your commitment to overcoming cravings for unhealthy foods. Repeat these affirmations to yourself:

1. "I release my cravings for unhealthy foods."
2. "I choose foods that nourish and energize my body."
3. "I enjoy making healthy choices."
4. "I am strong and in control of my cravings."
5. "Each day, I become healthier and more determined."

Step 9: Embracing the Benefits

1. **Visualize the Benefits of Healthy Choices**: Picture the positive changes that come from overcoming cravings and making healthy choices—feeling more energetic, improving your overall health, and experiencing greater well-being. Visualize yourself enjoying these benefits and feeling healthier and more in control.
2. **Feel the Empowerment**: As you visualize these benefits, feel a sense of empowerment and confidence. Know that you have the ability to maintain these healthy eating habits.

Step 10: Returning to Reality

1. **Return from the Visualization**: Imagine gradually returning from your visualization, bringing all the empowerment and clarity from the exercise with you. See yourself leaving the beautiful garden but knowing the benefits stay with you.
2. **Re-enter the Calming Place**: Visualize coming back to your calming place, feeling even more determined and ready to overcome cravings and make healthy choices.

Step 11: Returning to Wakefulness

When you are ready to end the session, imagine leaving your calming place, feeling refreshed and empowered. Count up from one to five. With each count, feel yourself becoming more alert and ready to engage in your day. By the count of five, open your eyes, feeling refreshed and in control.

Technique: The Power of Ho'oponopono

Step 1: Make Yourself Comfortable

Find a quiet, comfortable place where you can sit or lie down without being disturbed. Ensure the environment is free of distractions.

Step 2: Induction and Deepening

Use your favorite induction and deepening technique to enter a relaxed state.

Step 3: Entering the Visualization

1. **Imagine a Healing Sanctuary**: Picture yourself entering a serene and nurturing sanctuary, a place where you feel completely safe and at peace. This sanctuary is designed to help you connect with your body and heal from past behaviors. Visualize the sights, sounds, and feelings of this place, and let yourself fully immerse in its calming and healing energy.

2. **Describe the Sanctuary**: Think about the details of the sanctuary. Are there soft lighting, gentle music, and comfortable seating? How does it feel to be in this place of healing and forgiveness?

Step 4: Connecting with Your Body

1. **Visualize Your Body**: Imagine sitting or lying comfortably in the sanctuary, and then visualize your body in front of you as a separate entity. See your body as a cherished companion who has been with you through all your experiences.

2. **Feel the Connection**: As you visualize your body, feel a deep connection and appreciation for all it has done for you, despite the challenges and poor food choices.

Step 5: Apologizing to Your Body

1. **Speak to Your Body**: Using the principles of Ho'oponopono, speak directly to your body. Say the following phrases several times with sincerity and intention:

○ "I'm sorry for the way I have treated you."

○ "Please forgive me for the poor food choices and overindulgence."

○ "Thank you for all you have done to support me."

○ "I love you and I am committed to taking better care of you."

2. **Feel the Healing**: As you speak these phrases, imagine a warm, healing light surrounding both you and your body. Feel the power of these words to heal past wounds and create a foundation for better choices in the future.

Step 6: Visualizing Positive Change

1. **Visualize Healthy Choices**: Imagine yourself making healthy food choices and treating your body with respect and care. See yourself enjoying nutritious meals, staying hydrated, and engaging in physical activities that you love.
2. **Feel the Empowerment**: As you visualize these positive changes, feel a sense of empowerment and determination. Know that you have the ability to treat your body well and make choices that support your health and well-being.

Step 7: Positive Suggestions for Healing and Forgiveness

While in your healing sanctuary, give yourself some positive suggestions to reinforce your commitment to better self-care. Repeat these affirmations to yourself:

1. "I am sorry for my past choices, and I forgive myself."
2. "I am committed to treating my body with love and respect."
3. "I choose foods that nourish and heal my body."
4. "I thank my body for its resilience and strength."
5. "I love my body and am dedicated to its well-being."

Step 8: Embracing the Healing

1. **Visualize Embracing Your Body**: Imagine embracing your body, and feeling a deep sense of love, forgiveness, and gratitude. Visualize the healing light growing stronger and brighter, symbolizing your renewed commitment to self-care.
2. **Feel the Wholeness**: As you embrace your body, feel a sense of wholeness and peace. Know that you are now on a path of healing and positive change.

Step 9: Returning to Reality

1. **Return from the Visualization**: Imagine gradually returning from your visualization, bringing all the healing and forgiveness from the exercise with you. See yourself leaving the healing sanctuary but knowing the benefits stay with you.
2. **Re-enter the Calming Place**: Visualize coming back to your calming place, feeling even more determined and ready to take care of your body.

Step 10: Returning to Wakefulness

When you are ready to end the session, imagine leaving your calming place, feeling refreshed and empowered. Count up from one to five. With each count, feel yourself becoming more alert and ready to engage in your day. By the count of five, open your eyes, feeling refreshed and in control.

By incorporating these self-hypnosis techniques into your weight loss journey, you can develop healthy habits, stay motivated, and transform your relationship with food and your body.

Chapter 12: Breaking Addictions

Addictions can be incredibly difficult to overcome, but self-hypnosis can be a powerful ally.

Before we get into the ways to help break addictions, we need to clarify that some addictions are much more serious than others. Some can cause a body malfunction if you just try and stop whatever you're doing cold turkey.

I've worked with people addicted to everything from serious addictions like Crystal Meth to easier ones like nicotine (yes, that's easy) or sugar. The difference is that the serious ones can lead to a physical shutdown, even death. I personally won't work with someone with a serious addiction unless they are also receiving some other form of addiction treatment. If you are dealing with one of those serious addictions, feel free to reach out to me and we can discuss a therapy plan that includes additional resources to help you overcome that addiction at mindoverthebody.com

On the other hand, if you have an addiction that isn't going to cause your body to shut down, let's move on and break that addiction.

Some of the addictions that hypnosis is extremely effective in helping people overcome include, but are not limited to:

- Smoking or Vaping
- Light to moderate alcohol use
- Caffeine
- Video Games
- Social Media
- Television
- Sugar
- Shopping

- Gambling
- Work
- Pornography
- Hoarding

Now for those of you who are dealing with an addiction, you may have tried, and ultimately failed, breaking free from this behavior many times in the past, only to find yourself right back fully engaged in the pattern. That's usually the case when you try to use sheer willpower. Will-power is a conscious mind function, and we are going to need that to help us break these patterns, but willpower alone will lose almost every time to the imagination, and that's the deeper function of the subconscious mind.

As I discussed earlier in this book, one of the jobs that the subconscious has is to lead you toward pleasure and away from pain. Also remember that the subconscious doesn't know the difference between the past, present, or future. When you take both of these attributes and combine them together, it becomes an almost automatic response to keep you addicted to this behavior.

Let me give you an example. Let's say that when you got really upset in the past and went out to smoke a cigarette you felt a little calmer or less upset, even for just a moment. Your subconscious recorded that as pleasure. Now if the same thing or similar emotions presents itself again, it knows to give you the image and thought of smoking a cigarette to give you that momentary pleasure. Now apply that same thing to relaxing after a meal, with your morning coffee, socializing, talking on the phone, driving, or even boredom. The mind sets up all of these "pleasure patterns" to keep us in the cycle of addiction in order to bring us pleasure, even though the behavior is unwanted.

Another way certain patterns become an addiction is by subconscious programming we have received, sometimes even as children. Let's say your parents refused to let you get up from the table unless you finished all of your dinner, even if you were satisfied because "There are people starving in China!". Now I'm not sure how making someone eat beyond what they need helps end world hunger, but what I do know is that I've seen a lot of people that adopted an unhealthy relationship with food because of patterns when they were younger. Generational addictions are patterns that can form around a lot of behaviors. Eating, smoking, alcohol, sugar, hoarding, and a lot of others. You end up getting that perceived "pleasure", and in a lot of cases, you don't even know why.

And then there is video game addiction. As we talked about, the subconscious doesn't know the difference between what's real and what's imagined. When you put someone in front of a realistic-looking scene for hours, whether in real life or on the computer, the adrenaline and other physiological reactions start, like increased heart rate, sweating, and muscle tension. The reason those start is because the mind thinks those experiences are real, and to the subconscious, they are. Now take someone who plays these video games for hours long periods every day, they are creating a "pleasure pattern". That person can begin to crave those chemicals and patterns as almost an addiction of its own, and in some cases, at least at the moment, find the line between reality and fantasy become blurred.

So how can we break these addictions or pleasure patterns? You could try to go "cold turkey" but remember that imagination will win over willpower almost every time, so the first thing that needs to happen is to make sure you really want to break it, and the reason is for you. The deep desire to move past it for the betterment of YOUR life has to be there or the pattern and addiction will stay fully ingrained in you.

Next, if we are going to ask the subconscious to disconnect these "pleasure patterns" and replace them with new ones, we have to know what they are, what we can replace them with, disconnect the old ones, and give the mind new visions of the future when these old patterns are no longer present.

Let's start with the things you recognize as how your life would improve once this addiction has been disconnected. Come up with at least 5 positive outcomes.

Once I break this addiction to _________________________________, my life will immediately improve in the following ways:

1.)

2.)

3.)

4.)

Now look at your triggers and what they are connected to. What triggers you to engage in the pattern? It could be things like smoking after a meal, eating when upset, or drinking to calm down. Whatever your connections to the pattern are, list them below:

1.)

2.)

3.)

4.)

Recognizing the patterns or triggers is extremely important because you can't disconnect something unless you recognize the connection to start with.

Now make a list of the ways that this pattern has affected you in a negative way. Things like the damage to your health, the monetary cost, and time lost from doing what you really want. Whatever the negative effects have been, recognize them so that we can begin seeing this addiction for what it is, not a pleasure pattern.

This addiction to ______________________________________ has affected me and my life in the following negative ways:

1.)

2.)

3.)

4.)

Now before we get to the hypnosis to help us make those disconnections, it's time for some self-accountability. It's time to make a contract with yourself, but only if you are really ready to break this addiction once and for all. No statements like, "I'm going to try", "I'll give it a shot", we want to begin to get in the mindset of a person that doesn't have these issues to start with.

Let's create some pain now. Not physical pain, and not something that has a negative outcome. The pain I'm talking about is a way to hold yourself accountable for not keeping your work to yourself. Something that might be positive, but something you absolutely don't want to have to do over and over again. An example is a client of mine who wanted to quit drinking. She would go 5 or 6 days completely sober, then completely collapse and drink 2 bottles of wine in the evening one night. She came up with a way to hold herself accountable by saying, if I drink I have to attend an AA meeting. Now for some people that would be no big deal, and it could be a positive, but for her, she hated those meetings, she hated standing up and declaring "I'm an alcoholic". Not just one meeting, she had to go to a meeting every time she broke that promise to herself. That consequence, along with the hypnosis we did together was the last time she ever even wanted to drink. The consequence was stronger than the "pleasure" that the mind previously led her to. Now the pleasure was not having to go to an "AA" meeting. She adopted the mindset of a "Non-drinker" rather than the "AA" method of an identity that you are forever an alcoholic.

So think of something that is positive, but that you really don't want to do over and over again if you don't keep your word to yourself. Make it as painful as possible!

Now fill out your contract, and have someone witness it if you can. Then hang it up in a place so you have to see it as often as possible.

Here is a sample contract for you to write out.

Contract with myself

Contract start date _______________________

I _________________________________, enter into this contract with myself for the betterment of my life. I have previously engaged in a pattern of addiction to _______________________.

As of the date of this contract, I take on a new identity of a person that is free from _______________________., I declare myself to be a NON-_______________________.

I enter into this contract for myself and the following positive life changes that will happen as a result of being a NON-_______________________.

Recognizing that it is me who is solely responsible for creating and accepting these patterns in the past, should I not keep my contractual promises to myself, I commit to the following consequences for each time I engage in this past behavior.

1.)

2.)

3.)

4.)

I fully commit myself to my life improvement contract.

Signature_______________________ Date _______________

Witness_______________________ Date _______________

Now let's get the subconscious on team YOU where you can disconnect these past triggers and connections to this behavior of the PAST.

Technique: Breaking Addictions with the Control Center of the Mind

Step 1: Make Yourself Comfortable

Find a quiet, comfortable place where you can sit or lie down without being disturbed. Ensure the environment is free of distractions.

Step 2: Induction and Deepening

Use your favorite induction and deepening technique to enter a relaxed state.

At the end of your deepener, imagine that the stairs you descended, or the elevator you rode down on leads to a control room. The control center of your mind. Imagine seeing a control panel with an illuminated sign above it with the name of the addiction you are disconnecting. See all of the controls, dials, levers, cables, and buttons.

Step 3: Entering the Visualization

1. **Imagine the Control Center of the Mind**: Picture yourself entering a high-tech, serene control center within your mind. This control center is filled with advanced control panels, screens, and buttons that allow you to manage your thoughts, behaviors, and habits. Visualize the sights, sounds, and feelings of this place, and let yourself fully immerse in its empowering and calming energy.
2. **Describe the Control Center**: Think about the details of the control center. Are there glowing screens, control panels, and comfortable chairs? How does it feel to be in this place of control and power?

Step 4: Identifying the Addiction

1. **Visualize the Addiction Panel**: Imagine a specific control panel dedicated to the addiction you want to break. This panel has an illuminated sign above it with the name of the addiction. See the

various controls, dials, levers, cables, and buttons on this panel.

2. **Describe the Addiction**: Think about how this addiction looks and feels. Is it represented by a specific color, symbol, or image on the panel? How does it feel to acknowledge this addiction?

Step 5: Disconnecting the Addiction

1. **Visualize Disconnecting the Addiction**: Imagine walking up to the control panel and saying to yourself, "In the past, _________________ was connected to _________________, I now disconnect it."

○ For example, "In the past, smoking was connected to relaxation, I now disconnect it."

2. **Perform the Disconnection**: See yourself pulling the plug, turning a dial, or pushing a button to disconnect the addiction. Visualize the connection breaking and the addiction losing its power over you.

3. **Feel the Release**: As you disconnect the addiction, feel a sense of release and freedom. Imagine the addiction no longer having control over you, leaving you feeling empowered and in control.

4. Go through all of the past connections you came up with earlier and disconnect them all.

Step 6: Reprogramming with Positive Habits

1. **Visualize Reprogramming the Panel**: After disconnecting the addiction, imagine reprogramming the control panel with positive habits and behaviors. See yourself adjusting the controls, and setting new, healthy patterns.

2. **Feel the Positive Change**: As you reprogram the panel, feel a sense of positive change and growth. Imagine these new habits taking root

and becoming stronger each day.

Step 7: Positive Suggestions for Breaking the Addiction

While in your Control Center of the Mind, give yourself some positive suggestions to reinforce your commitment to breaking the addiction. Here are some general suggestions, but I have some addiction-specific ones listed below as well. Repeat these affirmations to yourself:

1. "I am free from ___________________."
2. "I control my thoughts and behaviors."
3. "I choose healthy habits and positive actions."
4. "I am strong and empowered to overcome this addiction."
5. "Each day, I become healthier and more in control."

Step 8: Returning to Reality

1. **Return from the Visualization**: Imagine gradually returning from your visualization, bringing all the empowerment and clarity from the exercise with you. See yourself leaving the Control Center of the Mind but knowing the benefits stay with you.
2. **Re-enter the Calming Place**: Visualize coming back to your calming place, feeling even more determined and ready to maintain your new, healthy habits.

Step 9: Returning to Wakefulness

When you are ready to end the session, imagine leaving your calming place, feeling refreshed and empowered. Count up from one to five. With each count, feel yourself becoming more alert and ready to engage in your day. By the count of five, open your eyes, feeling refreshed and in control.

Technique: River of Change Visualization for Breaking Addictions

Step 1: Make Yourself Comfortable

Find a quiet, comfortable place where you can sit or lie down without being disturbed. Ensure the environment is free of distractions.

Step 2: Induction and Deepening

Use your favorite induction and deepening technique to enter a relaxed state.

Step 3: Visualizing the River of Change

1. **Imagine the River of Change**: Picture yourself standing beside a serene, flowing river. This river represents the power of change and renewal. Visualize the sights, sounds, and feelings of this place, and let yourself fully immerse in its calming and transformative energy.
2. **Describe the River**: Think about the details of the river. Is it wide and gentle, or narrow and fast-flowing? Are there trees and flowers along its banks? How does it feel to be in this place of change and possibility?

Step 4: Identifying the Addiction

1. **Visualize the Addiction as Stones**: Imagine that each of your addictive behaviors or cravings is represented by a stone. These stones might be of different sizes and weights, symbolizing the impact of each addiction on your life.
2. **Describe the Stones**: Consider how these stones look and feel. Are some of them large and heavy, while others are smaller and lighter? How does it feel to acknowledge these addictions as burdens you've been carrying?

Step 5: Preparing to Release the Stones

1. **Visualize Holding the Stones**: Picture yourself picking up each stone and holding it in your hands. Feel the weight of the addiction and the impact it has had on your life. Acknowledge the stone and the addiction it represents.
2. **Feel the Readiness**: As you hold each stone, feel a sense of readiness to let go of the addiction and embrace change. Know that you have the strength and determination to release these burdens.

Step 6: Releasing the Stones into the River

1. **Visualize Releasing the Stones**: One by one, throw each stone into the flowing river. As each stone hits the water, watch it sink and be carried away by the current. As you release each stone, say to yourself, "I release _________________ and embrace positive change."

○ For example, "I release smoking and embrace positive change."

2. **Feel the Freedom**: As you release each stone, feel a profound sense of freedom and lightness. Imagine the addiction being washed away, leaving you feeling cleansed and renewed.

Step 7: Embracing New, Healthy Habits

1. **Visualize Planting Seeds**: After releasing the stones, imagine planting new seeds along the riverbank. These seeds represent healthy habits and positive changes you want to cultivate in your life. Visualize yourself planting them and nurturing their growth.
2. **Feel the Growth**: As you plant and nurture these seeds, feel a sense of growth and renewal. Imagine these new habits taking root and flourishing, symbolizing your commitment to a healthier and more fulfilling life.

Step 8: Positive Suggestions for Breaking the Addiction

While by the River of Change, give yourself some positive suggestions to reinforce your commitment to breaking the addiction. These are general suggestions, but I have some ideas for addiction-specific suggestions listed below. Repeat these affirmations to yourself:

1. "I am free from ___________________."
2. "I embrace positive and healthy changes in my life."
3. "I release old habits and welcome new, empowering behaviors."
4. "I am strong and capable of overcoming this addiction."
5. "Each day, I move closer to my healthiest, happiest self."

Step 9: Returning to Reality

1. **Return from the Visualization**: Imagine gradually returning from your visualization, bringing all the empowerment and clarity from the exercise with you. See yourself leaving the River of Change but knowing the benefits stay with you.
2. **Re-enter the Calming Place**: Visualize coming back to your calming place, feeling even more determined and ready to maintain your new, healthy habits.

Step 10: Returning to Wakefulness

When you are ready to end the session, imagine leaving your calming place, feeling refreshed and empowered. Count up from one to five. With each count, feel yourself becoming more alert and ready to engage in your day. By the count of five, open your eyes, feeling refreshed and in control.

Specific Suggestions for Different Types of Addictions

Alcohol Addiction

1. "I am free from the desire to drink alcohol."
2. "I find joy and relaxation in sober activities."
3. "I am healthier and happier without alcohol in my life."
4. "I enjoy being in control of my actions and decisions."
5. "I deserve a life free from alcohol and its negative effects."

Nicotine Addiction

1. "I am free from the need to smoke or use nicotine."
2. "I breathe easily and deeply without nicotine."
3. "I am proud of myself for choosing to live a smoke-free life."
4. "I am in control of my health and well-being."
5. "My body is healing and becoming stronger every day without nicotine."

Overeating (see the weight loss section as well)

1. "I listen to my body's hunger and fullness cues."
2. "I choose nutritious foods that nourish my body."
3. "I eat mindfully and with intention."
4. "I am in control of my eating habits and make healthy choices."
5. "I love and respect my body, and I treat it with care."

Caffeine Addiction

1. "I feel energized and awake without caffeine."
2. "I enjoy drinking water and other healthy beverages."
3. "I am free from my dependence on caffeine."

Social Media Addiction

1. "I enjoy my time away from social media."
2. "I am present and engaged in the real world."
3. "I control my social media usage, it does not control me."

Video Game Addiction

1. "I find joy and fulfillment in real-life activities."
2. "I limit my gaming time to maintain a balanced life."
3. "I am more than my achievements in video games."

Shopping Addiction

1. "I find satisfaction in non-material things."

2. "I make mindful and intentional purchases."
3. "I am free from the need to shop impulsively."
Sugar Addiction
1. "I crave healthy, nourishing foods."
2. "I enjoy the natural sweetness of fruits and vegetables."
3. "I am free from my dependency on sugary foods."

By incorporating these self-hypnosis techniques into your recovery journey, you can break free from addiction and build a healthier lifestyle.

If you find that you need additional support to break free from your addictions, visit mindoverthebody.com for more information.

Chapter 13: Business and Sales Success

In the world of business and sales, having the right mindset can make all the difference. Hypnosis and a positive outlook are powerful tools that can help you start your own business, climb the career ladder, or take your existing business to new heights. These techniques can help you break through mental blocks, stay focused, and build the confidence you need to succeed.

Starting Your Own Business

Thinking about starting your own business? It's exciting but can also be pretty scary. This is where hypnosis comes in handy. It can help you tackle those fears of failure, financial risks, and uncertainty that often hold people back. By using hypnosis, you can boost your self-belief and maintain a positive outlook, which is crucial when you're taking on something new. Visualizing your success and repeating positive suggestions can help you stay motivated and focused on your goals, even when things get tough.

Moving Up in Your Current Job

Want to advance in your career? Hypnosis can help you develop key skills like public speaking, leadership, and effective communication. If speaking in front of others makes you nervous, hypnosis can help you stay calm and confident. Visualizing successful presentations and interactions can improve your performance at work, leading to recognition, promotions, and new opportunities.

Boosting Your Existing Business

Already running a business? Hypnosis can help you stay on top of your game. Running a business comes with a lot of stress and challenges. Hypnosis can help you manage stress, make better decisions, and think creatively. Regular practice of hypnosis and positive suggestions can keep you aligned with your business goals, leading to steady growth and success.

The Power of a Positive Mindset

A positive mindset is essential in business and sales. It's what keeps you resilient, innovative, and successful. Hypnosis can help you reframe negative thoughts and replace them with empowering beliefs. For example, instead of thinking, "I can't close this deal," hypnosis can help you believe, "I am a confident and successful salesperson who can close any deal." This shift in mindset boosts your confidence and changes how you act and perform.

Having a positive mindset also helps you build strong relationships with clients and colleagues. It creates an environment of trust and collaboration, which is vital for business growth. Hypnosis can help you develop empathy, active listening skills, and emotional intelligence—all crucial for successful business interactions.

Let's take a look at a few people who have used the power of the mind to reach their goals in business and life.

Andrew Carnegie

Andrew Carnegie, the industrialist and philanthropist, was known to have used principles of autosuggestion, which are closely related to self-hypnosis. He believed in the power of positive thinking and mental conditioning to achieve success, a philosophy that has influenced countless business leaders.

Sir Winston Churchill

Although primarily known for his political career, Winston Churchill used self-hypnosis to manage stress and maintain his focus during the pressures of wartime leadership. His techniques have been adopted by many in the business world to handle high-stress situations and stay calm under pressure.

Richard Branson

Richard Branson, the founder of the Virgin Group, has openly talked about using meditation and visualization to help him stay focused and achieve his business goals. These practices are similar to hypnosis and have helped him maintain a positive and resilient mindset.

Tony Robbins

Tony Robbins, the motivational speaker and business strategist, who has had a huge impact on me personally uses visualization and neuro-linguistic programming (NLP) to help himself and others achieve peak performance. His techniques are widely used by business leaders to enhance their mental clarity and focus.

Bill Bartmann

Bill Bartmann, a billionaire entrepreneur, credited hypnosis for helping him recover from bankruptcy and rebuild his fortune. He used self-hypnosis to overcome fear, stay focused on his goals, and maintain a positive attitude, which played a significant role in his business turnaround.

Starting a New Business

Let's start off with starting your own business. It's a dream for a lot of people to work for themselves doing what they are passionate about. With changes coming to the world faster than any of us probably realize because of the advancements in artificial intelligence, now is a pretty good time to start thinking about starting something on your own. I've seen predictions that by the year 2030, AI will have replaced 30% of all jobs. Even if you think you are in a safe profession, chances are that AI will create some big changes down the road in almost all professions.

I've worked with a lot of people who wanted to start their own business or side hustle. While they can usually tell me what it is they want to do, and a basic outline of their plan, when I ask, why haven't you started yet, the avalanche of excuses starts flowing. If you "want" to start your own business, chances are you are going to look up a decade from now and either still "want" to, or "I wish I would have". I've heard all of the excuses, I don't have the money to start, once my kids get older I'll do it, I just need a little more knowledge or experience, I'm too old, too young, not talented enough, and the list goes on, and on.

I can personally guarantee you that there is someone who has less money, kids the same age, less knowledgeable, older, younger, or less talented than you are who is living the life you want right now. All because they took action in the direction of what they wanted.

When I ask people, what's the name of the business they want to start, most can't even answer that. It costs nothing to come up with a name (and you can choose to change it later if you want), but by naming it you've taken a step in the direction of making it happen. You can have business cards printed dirt cheap, an internet address is also a very minor investment. When you do those things they start putting you in the mindset of a business owner and often you find that doors you didn't even know existed start opening up for you. Start identifying as a business owner and you start adapting the mindset of a business owner even if it's a small step forward.

Look at all the excuses you are likely making right now, make a list, then throw it away. That list of excuses isn't going to help you in any way. Now make a list of all the things you could do today to start moving in that direction, and the next steps those small things could lead to tomorrow. There is a quote attributed to Jack Welch - Control your own destiny or someone else will.

Now let's look at a specific self-hypnosis technique for getting you in the right mindset to move forward with becoming that new business owner.

Technique: Visualizing Success for Starting a New Business and Taking Action

Step 1: Make Yourself Comfortable

Find a quiet, comfortable place where you can sit or lie down without being disturbed. Ensure the environment is free of distractions.

Step 2: Induction and Deepening

Use your favorite induction and deepening technique to enter a relaxed state.

Step 3: Visualizing the Business Success Center

1. **Imagine the Business Success Center**: Picture yourself entering a bright and inspiring space designed to help you visualize and achieve success in your new business. This space is filled with tools and resources that symbolize entrepreneurial success, such as business plans, computers, and charts of progress. Visualize the sights, sounds, and smells of this place, and let yourself fully immerse in its motivating energy.
2. **Describe the Center**: Think about the details of the Business Success Center. Are there whiteboards with plans, vision boards with goals, or shelves filled with inspiring books? How does it feel to be in this place of focus and ambition?

Step 4: Visualizing Your Successful Business

1. **Visualize Your Thriving Business**: Imagine seeing your business fully operational and thriving. Picture your workspace, your team, your products or services, and satisfied customers. Visualize the day-to-day operations running smoothly and your business achieving milestones.
2. **Describe the Details**: Think about the specifics of your business. What does the office or workspace look like? How do you interact with your team and customers? What milestones have you achieved?

How does it feel to see your business succeed?

Step 5: Identifying Key Actions

1. **Visualize Key Actions and Steps**: Picture a large, clear board in your Business Success Center. On this board, see the key actions and steps you need to take to get your business off the ground. These might include creating a business plan, networking, marketing, securing funding, and launching your product or service.
2. **Feel the Determination**: As you visualize these key actions, feel a sense of determination and clarity. Know that each step you take brings you closer to your business goals.

Step 6: Taking Inspired Action

1. **Visualize Taking Action**: Imagine yourself actively taking the steps needed to launch your business. See yourself making calls, attending meetings, working on your business plan, and executing your marketing strategy. Visualize each action being successful and bringing you closer to your goals.
2. **Feel the Momentum**: As you visualize taking these actions, feel a sense of momentum and progress. Imagine the excitement and satisfaction of moving forward and making your business a reality.

Step 7: Overcoming Obstacles

1. **Visualize Facing Challenges**: Picture yourself encountering challenges or obstacles on your business journey. See yourself handling these challenges with confidence and resilience, finding solutions, and continuing to move forward.
2. **Feel the Resilience**: As you visualize overcoming obstacles, feel a deep sense of resilience and adaptability. Know that you have the strength and resourcefulness to handle any challenge that comes your way.

Step 8: Positive Suggestions for Business Success

While in your Business Success Center, give yourself some positive suggestions to reinforce your confidence and determination. Repeat these affirmations to yourself:

1. "I am capable and confident in starting and running my business."
2. "I take action steps every day to achieve my business goals."
3. "I overcome challenges with resilience and creativity."
4. "I am committed to the success of my business."
5. "Each day, I move closer to achieving my business vision."

Step 9: Returning to Reality

1. **Return from the Visualization**: Imagine gradually returning from your visualization, bringing all the motivation and clarity from the exercise with you. See yourself leaving the Business Success Center but knowing the benefits stay with you.
2. **Re-enter the Calming Place**: Visualize coming back to your calming place, feeling even more determined and focused on your business goals.

Step 10: Returning to Wakefulness

When you are ready to end the session, imagine leaving your calming place, feeling refreshed and empowered. Count up from one to five. With each count, feel yourself becoming more alert and ready to take action. By the count of five, open your eyes, feeling refreshed and in control.

Technique: Transforming Setbacks and Failures into Feedback for Forward Movement

Step 1: Make Yourself Comfortable

Find a quiet, comfortable place where you can sit or lie down without being disturbed. Ensure the environment is free of distractions.

Step 2: Induction and Deepening

Use your favorite induction and deepening technique to enter a relaxed state.

Step 3: Visualizing the Mountain Summit

1. **Imagine the Mountain Summit**: Picture yourself standing at the base of a majestic mountain. This mountain represents your journey toward success, with each step and climb symbolizing your progress and challenges. Visualize the sights, sounds, and smells of this place, and let yourself fully immerse in its empowering and inspiring energy.
2. **Describe the Mountain**: Think about the details of the mountain. Are there snow-capped peaks, lush forests, or winding paths? How does it feel to be in this place of strength and determination?

Step 4: Identifying Setbacks and Failures

1. **Visualize the Trail Markers**: Imagine that along the mountain trail, there are markers representing your setbacks and failures. These markers can be rocks, signs, or symbols that stand out on your path. Each marker represents a challenge you've faced.
2. **Describe the Trail Markers**: Think about how these markers look. Are they large boulders, small stones, or wooden signs? How does it feel to see your setbacks and failures displayed as part of your journey?

Step 5: Reframing Setbacks and Failures

1. **Visualize Reframing the Markers**: Picture yourself standing in front of each trail marker. One by one, take a moment to reflect on each setback or failure. As you do, reframe each one as valuable feedback. Change the negative wording to positive insights and lessons learned.
2. **Feel the Transformation**: As you reframe each marker, feel a sense of clarity and empowerment. Recognize that each setback or failure is not a dead end but a stepping stone to greater success. Feel the weight of negativity lifting and being replaced with a sense of purpose and growth.

Step 6: Using Feedback to Move Forward

1. **Visualize Climbing the Mountain**: Imagine yourself using the feedback you've gathered to continue climbing the mountain. See yourself making adjustments, finding new routes, and using the lessons you've learned to navigate the path. Visualize the progress you make as a result of these actions.
2. **Feel the Momentum**: As you climb, feel a sense of momentum and forward movement. Imagine the excitement and satisfaction of making continuous improvements and moving closer to the summit.

Step 7: Embracing a Growth Mindset

1. **Visualize Embracing Growth**: Picture yourself fully embracing a growth mindset. See yourself welcoming challenges, learning from mistakes, and continuously growing stronger and more resilient with each step up the mountain.
2. **Feel the Empowerment**: As you embrace a growth mindset, feel a deep sense of empowerment and confidence. Know that you have the ability to turn any setback into an opportunity for growth and success.

Step 8: Positive Suggestions for Moving Forward

While climbing the mountain, give yourself some positive suggestions to reinforce your growth mindset and ability to use feedback effectively. Repeat these affirmations to yourself:

1. "I see setbacks and failures as valuable feedback."
2. "I learn and grow from every experience."
3. "I use feedback to continuously improve and move forward."
4. "I am resilient and adaptable in the face of challenges."
5. "Each day, I become stronger and more successful."

Step 9: Returning to Reality

1. **Return from the Visualization**: Imagine gradually returning from your visualization, bringing all the clarity and empowerment from the exercise with you. See yourself leaving the mountain summit but knowing the benefits stay with you.
2. **Re-enter the Calming Place**: Visualize coming back to your calming place, feeling even more confident and ready to use feedback to move forward.

Step 10: Returning to Wakefulness

When you are ready to end the session, imagine leaving your calming place, feeling refreshed and empowered. Count up from one to five. With each count, feel yourself becoming more alert and ready to take action. By the count of five, open your eyes, feeling refreshed and in control.

Technique: Overcoming Imposter Syndrome with the Achievement Visualization

Step 1: Make Yourself Comfortable

Find a quiet, comfortable place where you can sit or lie down without being disturbed. Ensure the environment is free of distractions.

Step 2: Induction and Deepening

Use your favorite induction and deepening technique to enter a relaxed state.

Step 3: Visualizing the Hall of Achievements

1. **Imagine the Hall of Achievements**: Picture yourself entering a grand, serene hall designed to showcase your achievements and help you overcome imposter syndrome. This hall is filled with bright light, beautiful decorations, and a calm atmosphere. Visualize the sights, sounds, and smells of this place, and let yourself fully immerse in its positive energy.
2. **Describe the Hall**: Think about the details of the hall. Are there tall pillars, beautiful artwork, or inspiring quotes on the walls? How does it feel to be in this place that celebrates your successes?

Step 4: Observing Your Achievements

1. **Visualize Your Achievements**: Imagine walking through the Hall of Achievements, where each success and accomplishment you've had is displayed. See awards, certificates, photos, and symbols representing your achievements.
2. **Describe the Achievements**: Think about the details of these displays. What achievements are highlighted? How do they look? How does it feel to see tangible evidence of your successes?

Step 5: Recognizing Your Worth

1. **Visualize Reading Positive Messages**: Imagine that along the hall, there are plaques and signs with positive messages about your skills, talents, and accomplishments. Take the time to read each one and let the words sink in.
2. **Feel the Validation**: As you read these positive messages, feel a growing sense of validation and worth. Recognize that your achievements are real and significant and that you deserve the recognition and success you have earned.

Step 6: Connecting with Your True Self

1. **Visualize a Mirror of Truth**: Imagine finding a large, beautiful mirror at the end of the hall. This mirror reflects your true self, showing not just your appearance, but also your inner qualities and strengths.
2. **Look into the Mirror**: As you gaze into the Mirror of Truth, see the confident, capable, and accomplished person you truly are. Let go of any doubts or negative thoughts, and embrace the reality of your abilities and achievements.

Step 7: Transforming Negative Thoughts

1. **Visualize Releasing Doubts**: Imagine that any lingering doubts or feelings of being an imposter are like dark clouds. See yourself blowing these clouds away, allowing the light of your true self to shine through.
2. **Feel the Transformation**: As the clouds of doubt dissipate, feel a deep sense of confidence and self-acceptance. Know that you are capable, worthy, and deserving of your success.

Step 8: Positive Suggestions for Overcoming Imposter Syndrome

While in your Hall of Achievements, give yourself some positive suggestions to reinforce your confidence and self-worth. Repeat these affirmations to yourself:

1. "I am deserving of my success and accomplishments."
2. "I recognize and celebrate my achievements."
3. "I am confident in my skills and abilities."
4. "I embrace my true self and let go of self-doubt."
5. "Each day, I become more confident and self-assured."

Step 9: Returning to Reality

1. **Return from the Visualization**: Imagine gradually returning from your visualization, bringing all the confidence and self-worth from the exercise with you. See yourself leaving the Hall of Achievements but knowing the benefits stay with you.
2. **Re-enter the Calming Place**: Visualize coming back to your calming place, feeling even more confident and at ease.

Step 10: Returning to Wakefulness

When you are ready to end the session, imagine leaving your calming place, feeling refreshed and empowered. Count up from one to five. With each count, feel yourself becoming more alert and ready to engage in your day. By the count of five, open your eyes, feeling refreshed and in control.

Technique: Eliminating Excuses

Step 1: Make Yourself Comfortable

Find a quiet, comfortable place where you can sit or lie down without being disturbed. Ensure the environment is free of distractions.

Step 2: Induction and Deepening

Use your favorite induction and deepening technique to enter a relaxed state.

Step 3: Visualizing the Excuse Elimination Screen

1. **Imagine the Excuse Elimination Screen**: Picture yourself in a comfortable room with a large, clear screen in front of you. This screen is designed to help you identify and eliminate the excuses that have been holding you back. Visualize the sights, sounds, and feelings of this place, and let yourself fully immerse in its empowering energy.
2. **Describe the Screen**: Think about the details of the screen. Is it a high-tech display, a simple whiteboard, or a holographic projection? How does it feel to be in this place where you can clearly see and address your excuses?

Step 4: Identifying Excuses

1. **Visualize the Excuses**: Think about the excuses or barriers that have held you back from starting your business. Imagine these excuses as small, dark clouds or labels appearing on the screen. Each excuse represents a specific fear, doubt, or limitation.
2. **Describe the Excuses**: Consider how these excuses look and feel. Are they large or small, faint or bold? How does it feel to see them displayed in front of you?

Step 5: Eliminating Excuses

1. **Eliminate Each Excuse**: For each excuse, say to yourself, "In the past, _____________________ was connected to _____________________, I now eliminate it."

○ For example, "In the past, fear of failure was connected to starting my business, I now eliminate it."

2. **Visualize Removing the Excuses**: See yourself on the screen taking action to remove these excuses. Picture your future self swiping away the clouds, erasing the labels, or simply watching them dissolve into nothingness. Watch as the image of your successful self becomes clearer and brighter with each excuse removed.

3. **Feel the Empowerment**: As you eliminate each excuse, feel a sense of empowerment and clarity. Imagine the weight of these excuses lifting, leaving you feeling lighter and more determined.

Step 6: Positive Suggestions for Success

While viewing this powerful image of your future success, give yourself some positive suggestions to reinforce your commitment to starting your business and not allow excuses to get in your way. Repeat these suggestions to yourself:

1. "I am free from excuses and fully committed to my success."
2. "I have the power to overcome any barrier or limitation."
3. "I take action with confidence and clarity."
4. "I am capable and ready to start my business."
5. "Each day, I move closer to achieving my business goals."

Step 7: Embracing the Vision of Success

1. **Visualize Your Successful Future**: Picture the screen now displaying a clear and bright image of your successful future self. See yourself

confidently running your business, achieving your goals, and feeling proud of your accomplishments.

2. **Feel the Success**: As you visualize this image, feel a deep sense of satisfaction and pride. Imagine the excitement and fulfillment of turning your dreams into reality.

Step 8: Returning to Reality

1. **Return from the Visualization**: Imagine gradually returning from your visualization, bringing all the clarity and determination from the exercise with you. See yourself leaving the room but knowing the benefits stay with you.
2. **Re-enter the Calming Place**: Visualize coming back to your calming place, feeling even more confident and ready to take action.

Step 9: Returning to Wakefulness

When you are ready to end the session, imagine leaving your calming place, feeling refreshed and empowered. Count up from one to five. With each count, feel yourself becoming more alert and ready to engage in your day. By the count of five, open your eyes, feeling refreshed and in control.

Growing Your Existing Business

Running an existing business comes with its own set of challenges and opportunities. Whether you're looking to expand your market reach, improve operational efficiency, or innovate new products, maintaining a positive and focused mindset is crucial. Self-hypnosis can be a powerful tool in this process, helping you to enhance your mental clarity, boost creativity, and manage stress effectively. Here's how self-hypnosis can assist in growing or expanding your business. Below I have some common ways to help you think clearly, calmly, and confidently as you work to expand your business.

Technique: Growth for an Existing Business

Step 1: Make Yourself Comfortable

Find a quiet, comfortable place where you can sit or lie down without being disturbed. Ensure the environment is free of distractions.

Step 2: Induction and Deepening

Use your favorite induction and deepening technique to enter a relaxed state.

Step 3: Visualizing the Business Growth Garden

1. **Imagine the Business Growth Garden**: Picture yourself entering a beautiful, thriving garden designed to symbolize the growth and success of your existing business. This garden is filled with vibrant plants, blooming flowers, and fruit-bearing trees, each representing different aspects of your business. Visualize the sights, sounds, and smells of this place, and let yourself fully immerse in its positive and nurturing energy.
2. **Describe the Garden**: Think about the details of the garden. Are there colorful flowers, tall trees, or gently flowing streams? How does it feel to be in this place of growth and abundance?

Step 4: Identifying Areas for Growth

1. **Visualize the Growth Areas**: Imagine walking through the garden and identifying specific areas that represent different aspects of your business that you want to grow. Each plant or tree symbolizes a particular area, such as marketing, customer relations, product development, or team efficiency.
2. **Describe the Areas**: Think about how these plants or trees look. Are some of them in need of more attention, while others are flourishing? How does it feel to see these areas of your business represented in the garden?

Step 5: Nurturing the Growth

1. **Visualize Nurturing the Plants**: Picture yourself taking action to nurture and grow these plants. This might involve watering, pruning, adding fertilizer, or providing support. See yourself actively working on these areas of your business, giving them the care and attention they need to thrive.
2. **Feel the Commitment**: As you nurture each plant, feel a sense of commitment and dedication. Imagine the positive impact your actions have on the growth and success of your business.

Step 6: Overcoming Obstacles

1. **Visualize Removing Obstacles**: Imagine encountering weeds, pests, or obstacles in your garden that represent challenges or setbacks in your business. See yourself effectively removing these obstacles, allowing the plants to grow freely and healthily.
2. **Feel the Empowerment**: As you remove each obstacle, feel a deep sense of empowerment and control. Know that you have the ability to overcome any challenges that arise and keep your business growing strong.

Step 7: Visualizing Abundant Growth

1. **Visualize the Garden in Full Bloom**: Picture your garden thriving and in full bloom, with each plant and tree representing a successful aspect of your business. See the vibrant colors, lush growth, and abundant harvest, symbolizing the growth and success of your business.
2. **Feel the Success**: As you visualize the abundant garden, feel a deep sense of satisfaction and pride. Imagine the excitement and fulfillment of seeing your business grow and succeed.

Step 8: Positive Suggestions for Business Growth

While in your Business Growth Garden, give yourself some positive suggestions to reinforce your commitment to growing your business. Repeat these affirmations to yourself:

1. "I am dedicated to growing my business."
2. "I take effective actions to nurture and expand my business."
3. "I overcome challenges with resilience and creativity."
4. "My business thrives and flourishes."
5. "Each day, my business grows stronger and more successful."

Step 9: Returning to Reality

1. **Return from the Visualization**: Imagine gradually returning from your visualization, bringing all the clarity and determination from the exercise with you. See yourself leaving the Business Growth Garden but knowing the benefits stay with you.
2. **Re-enter the Calming Place**: Visualize coming back to your calming place, feeling even more confident and ready to take action.

Step 10: Returning to Wakefulness

When you are ready to end the session, imagine leaving your calming place, feeling refreshed and empowered. Count up from one to five. With each count, feel yourself becoming more alert and ready to engage in your day. By the count of five, open your eyes, feeling refreshed and in control.

<u>Technique: Managing Stress While Growing an Existing Business</u>

Step 1: Make Yourself Comfortable

Find a quiet, comfortable place where you can sit or lie down without being disturbed. Ensure the environment is free of distractions.

Step 2: Induction and Deepening

Use your favorite induction and deepening technique to enter a relaxed state.

Step 3: Visualizing the Calm Oasis

1. **Imagine the Calm Oasis**: Picture yourself entering a serene and peaceful oasis designed to help you manage stress while growing your business. This oasis is filled with calming elements such as a tranquil pond, gentle breezes, and comfortable seating. Visualize the sights, sounds, and smells of this place, and let yourself fully immerse yourself in its soothing and rejuvenating energy.
2. **Describe the Oasis**: Think about the details of the oasis. Are there soothing waterfalls, soft grass, or warm sunlight? How does it feel to be in this place of relaxation and calm?

Step 4: Identifying Stressors

1. **Visualize the Stressors**: Think about the specific stressors related to growing your business. Imagine these stressors as small stones or pebbles that you carry in a backpack. Each stone represents a particular stress or challenge you are facing.
2. **Describe the Stressors**: Consider how these stones look and feel. Are some of them larger or heavier than others? How does it feel to acknowledge the weight of these stressors?

Step 5: Releasing the Stressors

1. **Visualize Releasing the Stones**: Picture yourself standing by the tranquil pond in the oasis. One by one, take each stone from your backpack and throw it into the pond. As each stone hits the water, watch as the ripples spread and then fade away, symbolizing the release of your stress.
2. **Feel the Lightness**: As you release each stone, feel a sense of lightness and relief. Imagine the burden of these stressors lifting, leaving you feeling more relaxed and at ease.

Step 6: Embracing Relaxation and Focus

1. **Visualize Embracing Calmness**: Imagine yourself sitting comfortably by the pond, feeling completely relaxed and calm. Focus on your breath, taking slow, deep breaths in and out. With each breath, feel a wave of relaxation washing over you, calming your mind and body.
2. **Feel the Focus**: As you embrace this state of relaxation, feel a sense of clarity and focus returning. Imagine yourself feeling refreshed and ready to tackle your business challenges with a clear mind and steady determination.

Step 7: Positive Suggestions for Managing Stress

While in your Calm Oasis, give yourself some positive suggestions to reinforce your ability to manage stress effectively. Repeat these affirmations to yourself:

1. "I release stress and embrace calmness."
2. "I handle business challenges with a clear and focused mind."
3. "I am in control of my emotions and reactions."
4. "I balance my business growth with relaxation and self-care."
5. "Each day, I become more resilient and at ease."

Step 8: Returning to Reality

1. **Return from the Visualization**: Imagine gradually returning from your visualization, bringing all the calmness and clarity from the exercise with you. See yourself leaving the Calm Oasis but knowing the benefits stay with you.
2. **Re-enter the Calming Place**: Visualize coming back to your calming place, feeling even more relaxed and ready to handle your business with confidence.

Step 9: Returning to Wakefulness

When you are ready to end the session, imagine leaving your calming place, feeling refreshed and empowered. Count up from one to five. With each count, feel yourself becoming more alert and ready to engage in your day. By the count of five, open your eyes, feeling refreshed and in control.

<u>Technique: Improving Leadership and Communication</u>

Step 1: Make Yourself Comfortable

Find a quiet, comfortable place where you can sit or lie down without being disturbed. Ensure the environment is free of distractions.

Step 2: Induction and Deepening

Use your favorite induction and deepening technique to enter a relaxed state.

Step 3: Visualizing the Leadership Conference Room

1. **Imagine the Leadership Conference Room**: Picture yourself entering a spacious, well-equipped conference room designed to enhance your leadership and communication skills. This room is filled with comfortable chairs, a large table, and advanced communication tools. Visualize the sights, sounds, and feelings of this place, and let yourself fully immerse in its inspiring and motivating energy.
2. **Describe the Room**: Think about the details of the conference room. Are there large windows letting in natural light, state-of-the-art technology, or inspiring artwork on the walls? How does it feel to be in this place of professional growth and development?

Step 4: Identifying Leadership and Communication Goals

1. **Visualize the Goals Board**: Imagine a large board in the room where you can write down your leadership and communication goals. These goals might include improving team motivation, enhancing clarity in communication, or fostering a collaborative work environment.
2. **Describe the Goals**: Consider how these goals look on the board. Are they written in bold, clear letters? How does it feel to see your

leadership and communication goals displayed in front of you?

Step 5: Enhancing Leadership Skills

1. **Visualize Leading a Meeting**: Picture yourself leading a successful meeting in the conference room. See yourself engaging with your team, confidently presenting ideas, and facilitating productive discussions. Visualize your team members responding positively to your leadership.
2. **Feel the Confidence**: As you lead the meeting, feel a sense of confidence and competence. Imagine yourself being clear, decisive, and supportive, inspiring your team to perform at their best.

Step 6: Improving Communication Skills

1. **Visualize Effective Communication**: Imagine yourself communicating effectively with your team members. See yourself listening actively, providing clear and concise instructions, and responding empathetically to feedback. Visualize the positive impact of your communication on your team's morale and productivity.
2. **Feel the Connection**: As you communicate, feel a sense of connection and understanding with your team. Imagine your words being understood and valued, creating a positive and collaborative work environment.

Step 7: Overcoming Communication Barriers

1. **Visualize Removing Barriers**: Picture any communication barriers, such as misunderstandings or conflicts, as obstacles in the room. See yourself addressing and removing these obstacles, clearing the way for open and effective communication.
2. **Feel the Clarity**: As you remove each barrier, feel a sense of clarity and ease. Imagine a smoother flow of communication, with everyone in the team feeling heard and understood.

Step 8: Positive Suggestions for Leadership and Communication

While in your Leadership Conference Room, give yourself some positive suggestions to reinforce your leadership and communication skills. Repeat these affirmations to yourself:

1. "I am a confident and effective leader."
2. "I communicate clearly and empathetically with my team."
3. "I inspire and motivate my team to achieve their best."
4. "I create a positive and collaborative work environment."
5. "Each day, my leadership and communication skills improve."

Step 9: Returning to Reality

1. **Return from the Visualization**: Imagine gradually returning from your visualization, bringing all the confidence and clarity from the exercise with you. See yourself leaving the Leadership Conference Room but knowing the benefits stay with you.
2. **Re-enter the Calming Place**: Visualize coming back to your calming place, feeling even more confident and ready to lead and communicate effectively.

Step 10: Returning to Wakefulness

When you are ready to end the session, imagine leaving your calming place, feeling refreshed and empowered. Count up from one to five. With each count, feel yourself becoming more alert and ready to engage in your day. By the count of five, open your eyes, feeling refreshed and in control.

Career Advancement

Maybe you are in a career where it isn't practical to start your own business, or it's just not your desire to do it, but you have a strong drive towards career advancement.

Not knowing what your specific career is, or what your ultimate goals are, makes it hard to create a one-size-fits-all technique, but let's start with the technique below:

Technique: Visualizing Career Advancement

Step 1: Make Yourself Comfortable

Find a quiet, comfortable place where you can sit or lie down without being disturbed. Ensure the environment is free of distractions.

Step 2: Induction and Deepening

Use your favorite induction and deepening technique to enter a relaxed state.

Step 3: Visualizing the Success Ladder

1. **Imagine the Success Ladder**: Picture yourself in a serene environment with a tall, sturdy ladder in front of you. This ladder represents your career journey and each rung symbolizes a step towards your career advancement. Visualize the sights, sounds, and feelings of this place, and let yourself fully immerse in its positive and motivating energy.

2. **Describe the Ladder**: Think about the details of the ladder. Is it made of wood or metal? Are the rungs labeled with different milestones or achievements? How does it feel to be in this place of growth and potential?

Step 4: Identifying Career Goals

1. **Visualize the Goal Rungs**: Imagine each rung of the ladder representing a specific career goal or milestone you want to achieve. These could include getting a promotion, leading a project, acquiring new skills, or receiving recognition for your work.
2. **Describe the Goals**: Think about how these goals look on the rungs. Are they labeled clearly with your ambitions? How does it feel to see your career goals mapped out in front of you?

Step 5: Climbing the Ladder

1. **Visualize Climbing the Ladder**: Picture yourself confidently climbing the ladder, step by step. With each rung you reach, feel yourself moving closer to your career goals. Imagine the excitement and satisfaction of progressing towards your aspirations.
2. **Feel the Progress**: As you climb, feel a sense of accomplishment and growth. Each step brings you closer to your desired career advancement, reinforcing your determination and commitment.

Step 6: Overcoming Obstacles

1. **Visualize Removing Barriers**: Imagine encountering obstacles on some rungs of the ladder. These obstacles could represent challenges or setbacks in your career. See yourself addressing and overcoming these barriers, clearing the way for your upward movement.
2. **Feel the Empowerment**: As you remove each barrier, feel a deep sense of empowerment and resilience. Know that you have the strength and capability to overcome any challenge that arises.

Step 7: Embracing Success

1. **Visualize Reaching the Top**: Picture yourself reaching the top of the ladder, where your ultimate career goal is achieved. See yourself in

your new role, receiving recognition, or leading a successful project. Visualize the positive impact of your achievements on your career and personal satisfaction.

2. **Feel the Success**: As you visualize this success, feel a deep sense of pride and fulfillment. Imagine the joy and confidence that comes with achieving your career goals.

Step 8: Positive Suggestions for Career Advancement

While visualizing your career success, give yourself some positive suggestions to reinforce your commitment and belief in your ability to advance. Repeat these affirmations to yourself:

1. "I am confident and capable of achieving my career goals."
2. "I take proactive steps towards my career advancement."
3. "I overcome challenges with resilience and determination."
4. "I am recognized and valued for my contributions."
5. "Each day, I move closer to achieving my career aspirations."

Step 9: Returning to Reality

1. **Return from the Visualization**: Imagine gradually returning from your visualization, bringing all the confidence and clarity from the exercise with you. See yourself leaving the Success Ladder but knowing the benefits stay with you.
2. **Re-enter the Calming Place**: Visualize coming back to your calming place, feeling even more determined and ready to take action towards your career goals.

Step 10: Returning to Wakefulness

When you are ready to end the session, imagine leaving your calming place, feeling refreshed and empowered. Count up from one to five. With each count, feel yourself becoming more alert and ready to engage in your career journey. By the count of five, open your eyes, feeling refreshed and in control.

Not knowing what your career is, or what your ultimate goals are makes it hard to create a one-size-fits-all technique, but let's start with an example below:

Technique: Nurturing Career Advancement in Your Success Garden

Step 1: Make Yourself Comfortable

Find a quiet, comfortable place where you can sit or lie down without being disturbed. Ensure the environment is free of distractions.

Step 2: Induction and Deepening

Use your favorite induction and deepening technique to enter a relaxed state.

Step 3: Entering the Visualization

1. **Imagine the Success Garden**: Picture yourself walking into a beautiful, lush garden—your Success Garden. This garden represents your career growth and potential. Visualize the sights, sounds, and smells of this place, and let yourself fully immerse in its vibrant and motivating energy.
2. **Describe the Garden**: Think about the details of the garden. Are there colorful flowers, tall trees, or gently flowing streams? How does it feel to be in this place of growth and possibility?

Step 4: Nurturing Your Success

1. **Explore the Garden**: Visualize yourself strolling through this vibrant garden. Notice the various plants and flowers representing different aspects of your career. Each plant symbolizes your skills, achievements, and aspirations.

2. **Identify Weeds (Excuses and Barriers)**: As you walk, you notice some weeds among the beautiful plants. These weeds represent the excuses or barriers that have held you back in your career. Acknowledge each weed as a specific excuse or barrier.

3. **Removing Weeds**: For each weed, gently pull it out and discard it. As you do, say to yourself, "In the past, _________________ was connected to _________________, I now remove it."

○ For example, "In the past, fear of failure was connected to advancing in my career, I now remove it."

4. **Planting New Seeds**: After clearing the weeds, plant new seeds in their place. These seeds represent your new, positive beliefs and goals. Visualize yourself planting them and imagine them growing strong and healthy. As you plant each seed, say to yourself, "I plant the seed of _________________ and watch it grow into _________________."

○ For example, "I plant the seed of confidence and watch it grow into career success."

Step 5: Watering and Caring for Your Garden

1. **Visualize Watering the Seeds**: Spend a few moments watering the new seeds and caring for the existing plants. This represents nurturing your new beliefs and goals. Imagine the water as a source of motivation, knowledge, and opportunities, helping your garden flourish.
2. **Feel the Growth**: As you water and care for your garden, feel a sense of satisfaction and progress. Visualize the garden flourishing, symbolizing your growing confidence, skills, and career advancement. See the flowers blooming and the plants thriving, reflecting your own professional growth.

Step 6: Positive Suggestions for Career Advancement

While in your Success Garden, give yourself some positive suggestions to reinforce your commitment to career growth. Repeat these affirmations to yourself:

1. "I am confident and capable of advancing in my career."
2. "I nurture my skills and talents to achieve my goals."
3. "I remove any barriers that hold me back."
4. "I am committed to my professional growth and success."
5. "Each day, I move closer to achieving my career aspirations."

Step 7: Returning to Reality

1. **Return from the Visualization**: Imagine gradually returning from your visualization, bringing all the confidence and clarity from the exercise with you. See yourself leaving the Success Garden but knowing the benefits stay with you.
2. **Re-enter the Calming Place**: Visualize coming back to your calming place, feeling even more determined and ready to take action towards your career goals.

Step 8: Returning to Wakefulness

When you are ready to end the session, imagine leaving your calming place, feeling refreshed and empowered. Count up from one to five. With each count, feel yourself becoming more alert and ready to engage in your career journey. By the count of five, open your eyes, feeling refreshed and in control.

By practicing these techniques regularly, you can reinforce your commitment to starting that new business, building the one you already have, or advancing in your career and eliminate the excuses that have been holding you back. These techniques help you tap into the power of your subconscious mind, setting a strong foundation for your professional growth and success.

Chapter 14: Manifesting Abundance

The concept of manifesting abundance and the Law of Attraction has gained widespread popularity in recent years, and for good reason. At its core, the Law of Attraction is the belief that our thoughts, feelings, and intentions have the power to shape our reality. This principle suggests that by focusing on positive thoughts and visualizing our desires, we can attract abundance and success into our lives. However, for this to work effectively, it is crucial to be crystal clear on what you want, and why you want it, and to truly believe that you already have it. Self-hypnosis can help you create this abundance in your life. Let's take a look at some of the key components of manifesting what we want in life:

Get Clear on <u>What</u> You Want

The first step in manifesting abundance is to be very specific about what you want. Vague or general desires won't yield the same results as clear, detailed intentions. Instead of simply wanting "more money," define the exact amount you wish to attract. Rather than hoping for "a better job," outline the specific position, company, and responsibilities you seek. The universe responds to precise requests, and clarity ensures that your energy is directed toward a tangible goal.

Understanding **<u>Why</u>** You Want It

Equally important is understanding why you want what you desire. Your motivations provide the emotional fuel that powers the Law of Attraction. When you connect deeply with your reasons, you generate stronger, more focused energy towards your goals. Ask yourself why achieving this goal matters to you. How will it improve your life? What benefits will it bring to those around you? The stronger and more positive your reasons, the more powerful your manifestation efforts will be.

Believing You **<u>Already Have It</u>**

One of the most critical aspects of manifestation and the Law of Attraction is the belief that you already possess what you desire. This mindset shift is essential because it aligns your vibrations with those of your goals. If you act and think as though you already have abundance, your subconscious mind begins to accept this reality, making it easier for you to attract the desired outcomes. Self-hypnosis and feeling the emotions associated with achieving your goals reinforce this belief.

The Reality of the Law of Attraction

The Law of Attraction is more than just wishful thinking; it's a real, powerful tool for creating the life you desire. Scientific studies have shown that our thoughts and emotions can significantly impact our physical reality. Positive thinking has been linked to better health outcomes, improved performance, and greater overall well-being. The principle behind the Law of Attraction is that by maintaining a positive, focused mindset, we can influence our circumstances and attract the resources, opportunities, and people needed to achieve our goals.

Now let's explore a specific technique to manifest what you want in life.

Technique: Activating the Law of Attraction and Manifesting Your Desires

Step 1: Make Yourself Comfortable

Find a quiet, comfortable place where you won't be disturbed. Sit or lie down in a relaxed position.

Step 2: Induction and Deepening

Use your favorite induction and deepening technique to enter a hypnotic state.

Step 3: Entering the Realm of Unlimited Potential

1. **Imagine a Gateway**: Visualize a beautiful, glowing gateway in front of you. This gateway represents the entrance to a realm of unlimited potential, beyond the limitations of the three-dimensional world.
2. **Step Through the Gateway**: See yourself confidently stepping through the gateway. As you cross the threshold, feel a sense of excitement and possibility. You are now in a place where anything is possible, where your desires can manifest freely.

Step 4: Exploring the Realm of Unlimited Potential

1. **Visualize Your Desires**: In this realm, you have the power to create anything you desire. Begin by visualizing your specific goals in vivid detail. See, hear, and feel what it's like to have already achieved them. Imagine every aspect of your success—how it looks, sounds, and feels.
2. **Engage All Senses**: Use all your senses to make the visualization as real as possible. If your goal is a new home, imagine the sight of the house, the smell of fresh paint, the sound of your footsteps on the floors, the feeling of the keys in your hand, and the emotions of joy and pride.

Step 5: Connecting with Your Why

Reflect on why you want to achieve these goals. Feel the deep emotional connection to your desires. Understand the positive changes they will bring to your life and the lives of those around you. Let this emotional connection strengthen your visualization.

Step 6: Believing You Already Have It

1. **Feel the Reality:** As you explore this realm of unlimited potential, believe that you already possess what you desire. Feel the emotions of success, satisfaction, and fulfillment. Embrace these feelings as your current reality.

2. **Positive Affirmations**: Repeat positive affirmations to reinforce your belief. Examples include:

○ "I am already living my dream life."

○ "I attract abundance and success effortlessly."

○ "I am worthy of all the good things that come my way."

Step 7: Anchoring Your Experience

1. **Create a Mental Anchor:** Choose a simple physical gesture, like touching your thumb and forefinger together, and associate it with the feelings of having achieved your desires. This anchor will help you recall and reinforce these feelings whenever you need them.
2. **Embrace Gratitude**: Feel gratitude for the abundance and success that is already yours. Expressing gratitude amplifies positive vibrations and attracts more of what you desire.

Step 8: Returning to Wakefulness

When you are ready to end the session, imagine yourself stepping back through the gateway and returning to the three-dimensional world. Count up from one to five. With each count, feel yourself becoming more alert and energized. By the count of five, open your eyes, feeling refreshed and confident.

By regularly practicing this visualization technique, you can activate the Law of Attraction and manifest your desires. This technique helps you tap into a realm of unlimited potential, where your goals are not only possible but already within your grasp. Stay committed to your vision, maintain a positive mindset, and watch as the universe responds to your focused, intentional energy, bringing your dreams to life.

Chapter 15: Managing Disease (From Cancer to Colds)

In my book, "Crushing Cancer...NOW!" I talk about how the power of our minds can do some pretty amazing things in our fight against disease. Everything from completely removing and preventing any side effects from treatments we may receive from disease treatment to actually healing from, or preventing advancement of the disease itself. While all diseases may not be able to go into full cure or remission, we can certainly improve our experience dealing with them and improve our outcomes. There is no separation between the body and the mind, but the big difference is that the mind is fully in charge of the body, we just see it the other way around most times.

I've worked with a lot of people who have been diagnosed with serious diseases, with breast cancer being the most common disease I've helped people overcome. I've worked with women whose doctors told them that all they could do was to help them manage the disease, and go into full remission. I can't prove that it was all the power of their minds, but at the same time, no one can prove it wasn't. The mind-body is designed for self-healing, it just needs to know what we want it to do.

The first step in fighting disease is to realize that Western medicine is generally going to list off every bad thing that anyone has ever experienced, even if it is only a fraction of the people receiving that treatment or dealing with that diagnosis. Your mind may fully accept those as fact through the nocebo effect, the unhelpful and destructive opposite of the placebo effect.

So the first thing we did was go over my "3 Main Rules of the mind" for dealing with any disease.

Rule #1 for all diseases: Accept the diagnosis, reject the prognosis (unless the prognosis is exactly the outcome you want)

Rule #2: You don't HAVE this ________________ disease, you have been DIAGNOSED with it.

Rule #3: All Negative Experiences are OPTIONAL

Let's start with taking a look at rule # 1 when dealing with any disease. The reality is that a prognosis is just someone's opinion, nothing more. If the prognosis isn't what you want to hear, don't be afraid to reject it outright, others have and by doing so created a completely different experience in their recovery. You have the power to create your own expectations and shape your own outcome.

A prognosis is basically an educated guess about what **might** happen based on other similar cases. But no two people are the same, and the journey doesn't have to be the same either. You're not a statistic. You're unique, and your body and mind have the potential to defy the odds, any odds.

If the prognosis you receive is negative, completely reject it in your mind, it doesn't serve you in any positive way. Accepting a bleak prognosis can lead to a self-fulfilling prophecy, where expecting the worst actually brings it about. Instead, we are going to choose to focus on positive outcomes that other people have already had. Imagine a future where you overcome the illness and live a full, healthy life. We take back control and refuse to let fear dictate the journey.

Now let's look at rule #2. Things we take on as part of our identity statement have tremendous power. "I am" or "I have" are statements that become part of you. That's something we never want when dealing with disease.

A diagnosis is just a label, not your identity. When you say, "I have cancer" or "I'm diabetic," it's like you're making the disease a part of who you are. But if you say, "I've been diagnosed with cancer" or "I'm living with diabetes," it puts a bit of distance between you and the illness. It's something you're dealing with, not something that defines you. To the mind, it makes a big difference. One way it's just part of you, the other way it becomes an unwelcome house guest that can be asked to leave. By thinking this way, you take back control of your story. You're not just someone with a disease; you're a person who's facing a challenge. This shift in perspective is powerful. It helps you focus on what you can do and your strengths, rather than what's wrong.

Finally, let's talk about rule #3, that all negative experiences, from chemo nausea, pain or discomfort, or any other symptom or side effect are completely optional to experience. All of those symptoms and side effects are created in the mind in reaction to some outside chemical or condition. You can change what the mind does and how it reacts. It might sound far-fetched, but I have seen it time and time again. In fact, in my practice, I have a near 100% success rate in helping people dealing with a diagnosis of disease have improved outcomes and experiences. Your mind has unlimited power to control any situation.

Whatever you are dealing with, from autoimmune disorders, cancers, viruses, and neurological disorders, to the common cold, the mind-body was designed for self-healing. By activating this power you can improve your outcome and experiences with these health challenges alongside conventional medical treatments.

Let's take a look at one of my favorite techniques. If you have worked with me in 1:1 sessions you have likely experienced the power of this session. Welcome to "The river of life."

Technique: The River of Life

Step 1: Make Yourself Comfortable

Find a quiet, comfortable place where you won't be disturbed. Sit or lie down in a relaxed position.

Step 2: Use your favorite induction and deepening technique to enter a hypnotic state. Get as deep as you can.

Step 3: Entering the River of Life

1. **Imagine the River**: Visualize yourself standing by the River of Life, a beautiful, serene river that flows with crystal-clear, healing water. See every detail that surrounds you. Imagine a sign that reads "Welcome to the River of LIFE" This river is filled with powerful, healing, restorative energy.
2. **Take a drink:** See yourself bending down and scooping up some of that water and feel it touch your lips as it enters your body. Feel the cool, refreshing water as it moves through your body, going straight to the areas that need healing or protection. Feel it bringing a sense of calm and peace.

Step 4: Absorb the Healing Energy

1. **Visualize Healing Water Entering Your Body**: Feel as it brings healing energy to every part of your body.
2. **Coating Your Body**: Visualize the water coating the inside of your body, creating a protective layer that shields you from the side effects of your treatment. Feel this protective coating strengthening you and providing relief from symptoms.

Step 5: Washing Away Disease

1. **See the Disease Being Washed Away:** Imagine the water flowing through your body, collecting all the disease, toxins, and negative energy. See these impurities being washed away by the powerful current of the river.
2. **Feel the Cleansing:** As the water flows through you, feel it cleansing every cell, tissue, and organ. Visualize the disease leaving your body, being carried away by the healing water.

Step 6: Positive Suggestions for Healing

While this healing water flows through you, give yourself some positive suggestions to reinforce your healing process. Repeat these affirmations to yourself:

1. "My body is absorbing the healing energy of the River of Life."
2. "This healing water protects me from all side effects and restores my health."
3. "Every cell in my body is being cleansed and rejuvenated."
4. "I am strong, healthy, and free from disease."
5. "My body heals quickly and efficiently, washing away all illness."
6. "I am surrounded by the powerful, restorative energy of the River of Life."

Step 7: Returning to Conscious Awareness

When you are ready to end the session, imagine yourself stepping out of the river, feeling revitalized and cleansed. Count up from one to five. With each count, feel yourself becoming more alert and energized. By the count of five, open your eyes, feeling refreshed and confident in your healing.

Technique: Boosting the Immune System

Step 1: Make Yourself Comfortable

Find a quiet, comfortable place where you can sit or lie down without being disturbed. Ensure the environment is free of distractions.

Step 2: Induction and Deepening

Use your favorite induction and deepening technique to enter a relaxed state.

Step 3: Entering the Visualization

1. **Imagine a Comfortable Healing Room**: Picture yourself in a comfortable, serene room designed for healing. This room is filled with soft lighting, cozy furniture, and a calming atmosphere. Visualize the sights, sounds, and feelings of this place, and let yourself fully immerse in its soothing and rejuvenating energy.
2. **Describe the Healing Room**: Think about the details of the room. Are there plush cushions, gentle music, and perhaps the scent of lavender or other calming aromas? How does it feel to be in this place of safety and comfort?

Step 4: Visualizing the Spark of Light

1. **Visualize the Spark of Light**: Imagine a tiny spark of white light at the core of your body, near your heart. This spark represents your immune system's energy and strength. See it glowing brightly and steadily.
2. **Describe the Spark**: Think about how this spark looks and feels. Is it warm and radiant, with a calming energy? How does it feel to visualize this powerful light within you?

Step 5: Growing the Light

1. **Visualize the Light Expanding**: Imagine the spark of white light growing and expanding with each breath you take. See it spreading from your core throughout your entire body, reaching every cell and organ. As it expands, it energizes and boosts your immune system.
2. **Feel the Strength**: As the light expands, feel a sense of strength and vitality growing within you. Imagine your immune system becoming more robust and effective at fighting off disease.

Step 6: Cleansing and Healing

1. **Visualize the Light Clearing Toxins**: Picture the growing light surrounding and dissolving any toxins or pathogens in your body. See these dark spots or clouds being cleared away by the powerful light, leaving your body clear and healthy.
2. **Feel the Healing**: As the light clears away toxins, feel a deep sense of healing and purification. Imagine your body becoming more balanced and resilient.

Step 7: Positive Suggestions for Immune System Health

While in your healing room, give yourself some positive suggestions to reinforce your commitment to a strong immune system. Repeat these affirmations to yourself:

1. "My immune system is strong and effective."
2. "Every part of my immune system works perfectly to protect me."
3. "I am healthy, vibrant, and resilient."
4. "My body heals quickly and efficiently."
5. "I am filled with energy and vitality."

Step 8: Embracing the Healing

1. **Visualize Embracing Your Immune System**: Imagine embracing

your immune system with gratitude and appreciation. Visualize the healing light growing stronger and brighter, symbolizing your renewed commitment to health.

2. **Feel the Empowerment**: As you embrace your immune system, feel a sense of empowerment and confidence. Know that you are now on a path of healing and positive change.

Step 9: Returning to Reality

1. **Return from the Visualization**: Imagine gradually returning from your visualization, bringing all the healing and strength from the exercise with you. See yourself leaving the comfortable healing room but knowing the benefits stay with you.
2. **Re-enter the Calming Place**: Visualize coming back to your calming place, feeling even more determined and ready to maintain a strong immune system.

Step 10: Returning to Wakefulness

When you are ready to end the session, imagine leaving your calming place, feeling refreshed and empowered. Count up from one to five. With each count, feel yourself becoming more alert and ready to engage in your day. By the count of five, open your eyes, feeling refreshed and in control.

Technique: Visualizing Positive Outcomes

Step 1: Make Yourself Comfortable

Find a quiet, comfortable place where you can sit or lie down without being disturbed. Ensure the environment is free of distractions.

Step 2: Induction and Deepening

Use your favorite induction and deepening technique to enter a relaxed state.

Step 3: Entering the Visualization

1. **Imagine a Healing Forest**: Picture yourself entering a beautiful, serene forest. This forest is filled with tall trees, lush greenery, and the gentle sounds of nature. Visualize the sights, sounds, and feelings of this place, and let yourself fully immerse in its healing and rejuvenating energy.
2. **Describe the Forest**: Think about the details of the forest. Are there tall trees, a gentle stream, and birds singing? How does it feel to be in this place of peace and healing?

Step 4: Visualizing a Healing Light

1. **Visualize a Healing Light**: Imagine a warm, glowing light above you. This light represents healing energy and positivity. See the light gently descending and surrounding your entire body.
2. **Describe the Light**: Think about how this light looks and feels. Is it a soft, golden glow with a warm and comforting energy? How does it feel to be bathed in this healing light?

Step 5: Absorbing the Healing Light

1. **Visualize the Light Entering Your Body**: Imagine the healing light penetrating your skin and entering your body. See it flowing through your bloodstream, reaching every cell and organ. As it flows, it brings healing, strength, and positive energy.
2. **Feel the Healing**: As the light flows through you, feel a sense of healing and rejuvenation. Imagine the light repairing damaged cells, boosting your immune system, and filling you with vitality.

Step 6: Focusing on Positive Outcomes

1. **Visualize Positive Outcomes**: Picture yourself fully healed and healthy. See yourself engaging in activities you love, feeling energetic and vibrant. Imagine the joy and relief of being free from disease.
2. **Feel the Positivity**: As you visualize these positive outcomes, feel a deep sense of hope and confidence. Know that your body has the ability to heal and that positive outcomes are within your reach.

Step 7: Positive Suggestions for Healing

While in your healing forest, give yourself some positive suggestions to reinforce your commitment to healing. Repeat these affirmations to yourself:

1. "My body has a remarkable ability to heal and restore itself."
2. "I am becoming healthier and stronger every day."
3. "I am filled with positive energy and healing light."
4. "I trust in my body's ability to recover fully."
5. "I am grateful for the healing process and the positive outcomes it brings."

Step 8: Embracing the Healing

1. **Visualize Embracing Your Health**: Imagine embracing your body with gratitude and appreciation. Visualize the healing light growing

stronger and brighter, symbolizing your renewed commitment to health.

2. **Feel the Empowerment**: As you embrace your health, feel a sense of empowerment and confidence. Know that you are on a path of healing and positive change.

Step 9: Returning to Reality

1. **Return from the Visualization**: Imagine gradually returning from your visualization, bringing all the healing and positivity from the exercise with you. See yourself leaving the healing forest but knowing the benefits stay with you.

2. **Re-enter the Calming Place**: Visualize coming back to your calming place, feeling even more determined and ready to support your body's healing process.

Step 10: Returning to Wakefulness

When you are ready to end the session, imagine leaving your calming place, feeling refreshed and empowered. Count up from one to five. With each count, feel yourself becoming more alert and ready to engage in your day. By the count of five, open your eyes, feeling refreshed and in control.

Technique: Overcoming the Fear of Recurrence

Step 1: Make Yourself Comfortable

Find a quiet, comfortable place where you can sit or lie down without being disturbed. Ensure the environment is free of distractions.

Step 2: Induction and Deepening

Use your favorite induction and deepening technique to enter a relaxed state.

Step 3: Entering the Visualization

1. **Imagine a Safe Space**: Picture yourself in a safe, serene space of your choosing. This could be a comfortable room, a tranquil beach, or a lush forest. Visualize the sights, sounds, and feelings of this place, and let yourself fully immerse in its calming and protective energy.
2. **Describe the Safe Space**: Think about the details of your safe space. Are there soft lighting, gentle music, or the soothing sound of waves? How does it feel to be in this place of safety and comfort?

Step 4: Visualizing a Protective Shield

1. **Visualize a Protective Shield**: Imagine a warm, glowing shield of light surrounding your entire body. This shield represents protection from fear and anxiety. See it glowing brightly and steadily, keeping you safe and calm.
2. **Describe the Shield**: Think about how this shield looks and feels. Is it a soft, golden glow with a warm and comforting energy? How does it feel to be surrounded by this protective shield?

Step 5: Addressing the Fear

1. **Visualize the Fear**: Imagine the fear of recurrence as a dark cloud outside your protective shield. See it swirling and trying to get closer, but unable to penetrate the shield.
2. **Acknowledge the Fear**: Acknowledge the fear by saying to yourself, "I see you, and I understand why you are here. But you cannot control me."

Step 6: Dissolving the Fear

1. **Visualize the Shield Growing Stronger**: Imagine the protective shield growing stronger and brighter, pushing the dark cloud of fear further away. See the fear dissolving and fading into nothingness.

2. **Feel the Empowerment**: As the fear dissolves, feel a deep sense of empowerment and calm. Know that you have the strength and resilience to keep the fear at bay.

Step 7: Positive Suggestions for Overcoming Fear

While in your safe haven, give yourself some positive suggestions to reinforce your commitment to overcoming the fear of recurrence. Repeat these affirmations to yourself:

1. "I am safe and protected from fear."
2. "I have the strength and resilience to overcome any challenge."
3. "I trust in my body's ability to stay healthy and strong."
4. "I focus on the present moment and live with confidence and peace."
5. "Each day, I become more empowered and fearless."

Step 8: Embracing the Calm

1. **Visualize Embracing the Calm**: Imagine embracing your body with gratitude and appreciation. Visualize the protective shield growing stronger and brighter, symbolizing your renewed commitment to living without fear.
2. **Feel the Peace**: As you embrace the calm, feel a sense of peace and confidence. Know that you are on a path of positive change and empowerment.

Step 9: Returning to Reality

1. **Return from the Visualization**: Imagine gradually returning from your visualization, bringing all the calm and strength from the exercise with you. See yourself leaving the safe haven but knowing the benefits stay with you.
2. **Re-enter the Calming Place**: Visualize coming back to your calming place, feeling even more determined and ready to live without fear.

Step 10: Returning to Wakefulness

When you are ready to end the session, imagine leaving your calming place, feeling refreshed and empowered. Count up from one to five. With each count, feel yourself becoming more alert and ready to engage in your day. By the count of five, open your eyes, feeling refreshed and in control.

Regardless of what "Dis-ease" you have been diagnosed with, you have incredible power to improve your own outcome. I see remarkable healing happening every day. People who have recovered or who have a better outcome than you don't possess any secret power that you don't have. They are just using theirs in a better way.

For more information on my cancer-specific therapies, visit www.themindovercancer.com[1]

For other diseases and conditions, you can get more information at www.mindoverthebody.com[2]

---

1. http://www.themindovercancer.com

2. http://www.mindoverthebody.com

Chapter 16: Chronic Stress

Stress is a part of life, but living in a constant state of stress is a problem for a lot of people these days. Not only is living in that state of stress mentally draining, but it can also lead to physical disease.

We talked earlier about the sympathetic nervous system and how that is the part of the nervous system responsible for the "Flight, Fight, or Freeze" response. The sympathetic nervous system has helped since the beginning of human existence to stay alive, but it is not intended to stay activated all of the time. It's meant for immediate danger situations and then it's supposed to deactivate and turn things back over to the parasympathetic nervous system once the danger has passed.

When we live in states of constant chronic stress, the sympathetic nervous system never fully disengages. It continues to pump out those stress hormones and chemicals. Those chemicals, while helpful in flight, fight, or freeze situations, create an atmosphere in the body that is the perfect environment for disease to form.

Regardless of the source of that initial stress, whether it's work, family, self-image, relationships, or just general life struggles, finding ways to reduce that stress and disengage that sympathetic nervous system is vital for your overall health.

The following technique is about putting those stressful situations away for a while. They can stay locked up until you are refreshed and ready to deal with them one at a time.

For chronic stress, I would recommend getting into a hypnotic state 2-3 times a day for 10-15 minutes until you find yourself naturally staying in a more stress-free mindset.

PERSONAL TRANSFORMATION FROM WITHIN: THE POWER OF SELF HYPNOSIS FOR LASTING CHANGE

It doesn't have to control you. Learn how to use self-hypnosis to relax, recharge, and handle stress more effectively. This chapter provides practical tools to help you maintain a sense of calm and balance, no matter what life throws your way.

<u>Technique: Locking Away Stress and Embracing Calm</u>

Step 1: Make Yourself Comfortable

Find a quiet, comfortable place where you won't be disturbed. Sit or lie down in a relaxed position.

Step 2: Induction and Deepening

Use your favorite induction and deepening technique to enter a hypnotic state.

Step 3: Visualizing the Box

1. **Imagine a Safe Space**: Picture yourself in a safe, serene environment where you feel completely at ease. This could be a beach, a forest, or a cozy room.
2. **See the Stress Box**: Visualize a sturdy, secure box in front of you. This box is where you will lock away your stress. It's strong and has a heavy, secure lock.

Step 4: Placing Stress into the Box

1. **Identify Your Stress**: Think about the things that are causing you stress. Imagine each stressor as a tangible object you can hold in your hands.
2. **Place Stress into the Box**: One by one, take each stressor and place it into the box. See yourself putting the lid on the box after each stressor, feeling a sense of relief as you do.
3. **Locking the Box**: Once all your stressors are inside, visualize yourself locking the box securely. Feel the weight lifting off your shoulders as you hear the click of the lock.

Step 5: Embracing Calm and Peace

1. **Focus on Calm**: Now, shift your focus to the calmness of your safe space. Take deep breaths, inhaling peace and exhaling any remaining tension.
2. **Feel the Peace**: Visualize a warm, soothing light surrounding you. This light represents calm and peace, enveloping your entire body and mind.
3. **Gratitude Visualization**: Think about the things you are grateful for. Visualize these moments, people, or experiences filling your heart with warmth and happiness.

Step 6: Positive Suggestions for Relaxation

While in this state of calm, give yourself some positive suggestions to reinforce your relaxation. Repeat these affirmations to yourself:

1. "I am calm and at peace in this moment."
2. "I have locked away my stress and can now fully relax."
3. "I am surrounded by a warm, soothing light that brings me tranquility."
4. "I am grateful for the positive things in my life and they bring me joy."
5. "I release all tension and embrace calm and serenity."
6. "I am in control of my stress and can choose peace at any time."

Step 7: Returning to Awareness

When you are ready to end the session, imagine yourself leaving your safe space, carrying a sense of calm and peace with you. Count up from one to five. With each count, feel yourself becoming more alert and energized. By the count of five, open your eyes, feeling refreshed and relaxed.

Chapter 17: Healing Past Trauma

Everyone has had some type of trauma happen over the course of their life, but the severity of that trauma and the way it's processed varies significantly from person to person.

We all have our own version of reality. What's real to you may not be the way I interpret the same situation at all. This can be extremely important when it comes to releasing past trauma.

Imagine two people who both went through similar experiences of childhood abuse. For the first person, the trauma sticks with them throughout their life, affecting their relationships and daily life, even though the event may have happened years, or even decades ago. They might often feel anxious and have trouble trusting others, always expecting the worst because of what they experienced. Their past abuse is a heavy burden that they carry, making it hard for them to move forward and find peace.

On the other hand, let's look at the second person who has a different take on their past. While the abuse was undeniably painful, they see themselves as a survivor who has become stronger because of it. They use their experience to fuel his or her determination and empathy, becoming an advocate for others who've been through similar situations. They find purpose in their pain, channeling it into positive actions and personal growth. While both people faced similar abuse, their subjective realities led them down very different paths—one burdened by the past and the other empowered by it.

When we experience past traumas, an emotion can become linked to that past event. That emotional attachment can often be the key to releasing the effects of that past trauma. While we can't erase past memories, we can disconnect ourselves from the emotions of those past events.

PERSONAL TRANSFORMATION FROM WITHIN: THE POWER OF SELF HYPNOSIS FOR LASTING CHANGE

I've seen clients who go from completely breaking down into intense emotions when recalling a past traumatic event to complete emotional detachment from that event in 30 minutes. The event remains in the memory, but they find that they just can't recall the emotion that used to be attached to it, and as a result, the mind processes and stores that event differently from that point forward. The mainstream belief is that to heal trauma you have to spend years in talk therapy reliving the event over and over and somehow bring a little closure to that event. The exact opposite has been my experience. I've helped people overcome traumas without them even telling me what the traumatic event was, to begin with. As long as I guide them through the techniques, they can make those disconnections all on their own. To be clear, I think that for some people having someone to talk with is a beneficial thing, I also think that there are better things to talk about than a past trauma that can be disconnected a lot more effectively.

Now, I use a lot of advanced techniques when working with trauma. In my practice, I almost always use a combination of regression to cause hypnotherapy, neuro-linguistic programming (NLP), and eye movement integration therapy (EMI), but self-hypnosis can also be an effective way for you to begin making these disconnections on your own. With past trauma, it is usually a good idea to use self-hypnosis alongside some more advanced techniques for the best overall results.

So how do we go about disconnecting this past event from the emotions that have anchored to it? The first step in self-hypnosis is to ask yourself all of the ways that holding on to this past event has negatively affected you. Is it affecting your emotional state, feelings of self-worth, relationships, physical health, or just overall well-being? Identifying how it is affecting you gives a starting point for healing.

This past emotional event has affected my life in the following negative ways:

1.)

2.)

3.)

4.)

Now ask yourself, on a scale of 0 to 10 how intense is my emotional connection to this event? (0 being it doesn't affect me at all, and 10 being extreme pain or emotions). Knowing where we are starting from is important for us to measure progress in releasing it.

1 2 3 4 5 6 7 8 9 10

When you are able to resolve this trauma how will that positively affect your life?

1.)

2.)

3.)

4.)

What are the underlying emotions that are attached to this event or experience? Is it anger, sadness, guilt, shame, or fear? List your own emotions so that we can find, and ultimately disconnect them.

1.)

2.)

3.)

4.)

Earlier in the book I talked about secondary benefits and how if they exist the chances of success using any form of hypnosis are low. So, ask yourself, Is there any reason to continue holding on to this event, emotions, or negative effects?

When you are ready to start releasing this past trauma, use the technique below. Again, if you feel that you could benefit from guidance in your healing, go to mindoverthebody.com for additional resources.

Technique: Releasing Past Trauma

Step 1: Make Yourself Comfortable

Find a quiet, comfortable place where you won't be disturbed. Sit or lie down in a relaxed position.

Step 2: Induction and Deepening

Use your favorite induction and deepening technique to enter a hypnotic state.

Step 3: Establishing a Safe Space

1. **Visualize Your Safe Space:** Imagine a place where you feel completely safe and at peace. This could be a serene beach, a cozy room, or a beautiful garden. Fill this space with details that make you feel calm and secure.
2. **Anchor Your Safe Space:** Know that you can return to this safe space at any time during the visualization if emotions become too intense. This is your sanctuary where you can always find comfort and peace.

Step 4: Going Back in Time

1. **Visualize a Time Machine:** Imagine a time machine in your safe space. See yourself stepping into it, knowing it will take you back to the root of your trauma.
2. **Set the Destination:** Set the time machine to the specific moment when the traumatic event occurred. As the machine activates, feel yourself traveling back in time, yet remaining calm and detached.

Step 5: Observing the Event

1. **Arrive at the Scene:** As the time machine stops, find yourself at the

scene of the traumatic event, but as an observer, dissociated from the emotions. You are there as your current self, watching from a safe distance.

2. **Observe Without Judgment**: See the event unfold without getting emotionally involved. Observe your younger self experiencing the trauma.

Step 6: Offering Comfort and Support

1. **Approach Your Younger Self**: When you feel ready, gently approach your younger self in the scene. Imagine giving them comfort and reassurance. Let them know that they are not alone and that they are safe now.

2. **Speak to Those Involved**: If there are other people in the scene, imagine saying what you need to say to them. This could be expressing your feelings, setting boundaries, or simply stating your truth.

Step 7: Letting Go

1. **Ask the Important Question**: Turn to your younger self and ask, "Is there any reason to hold onto this any longer, knowing that it is affecting me negatively today?"

2. **Visualize Release**: Imagine the trauma as a heavy weight or dark cloud. Visualize it lifting away from your younger self and from you. See it dissolving into the air, leaving you both feeling lighter and free.

Step 8: Returning to the Safe Space

1. **Return to the Time Machine**: Guide your younger self to the time machine with you, and set the destination to your safe space.

2. **Re-enter the Safe Space**: Step out of the time machine and back into your safe space. Feel the comfort and peace of this sanctuary enveloping you.

Step 9: Positive Suggestions for Healing

While in your safe space, give yourself some positive suggestions to reinforce your release of the trauma. Repeat these affirmations to yourself:

1. "I am free from the burden of my past trauma."
2. "I am safe, secure, and at peace."
3. "I have released the negative emotions and embraced healing."
4. "I am strong, resilient, and capable of moving forward."
5. "My past does not define me; I choose my future."

Step 10: Returning to Wakefulness

When you are ready to end the session, imagine leaving your safe space, feeling light and free. Count up from one to five. With each count, feel yourself becoming more alert and energized. By the count of five, open your eyes, feeling refreshed and empowered.

After your self-hypnosis session, ask yourself again, on a scale of 0-10 how much does this past trauma affect me emotionally now? Can I see this past event differently? Was there any new information I was able to take from this experience? Is there any positive that I can take from this? Even small improvements are a success, so celebrate it and keep moving forward.

By regularly practicing this visualization technique, you can work through past trauma, offering comfort to your younger self and releasing the negative emotions associated with the event. This technique helps you process the trauma in a safe, controlled way, allowing you to move forward with a sense of peace and healing. Stay committed to this practice, maintain a positive mindset, and embrace the freedom from your past.

Chapter 18: Helping Children with Self-Hypnosis

In this section, we will be talking about how you can use hypnosis to help your children overcome common childhood issues. You will become their hypnotist learning how to guide them to the desired outcome.

When it comes to hypnosis, kids are like little sponges, ready to soak up all the benefits. Seriously, they're naturals at this because they are always in a little bit of a trance state to start with! Unlike adults, who often overthink everything and have a million doubts, kids just go with the flow. This makes hypnosis extremely effective for them, whether it's for dealing with anxiety, getting over fears, or even tackling things like bedwetting.

One big reason kids are so easy to hypnotize is their amazing imagination. Have you ever watched a child play? They can turn a cardboard box into a spaceship and believe it with all their heart. This imaginative power is perfect for hypnosis. When you ask a child to picture a calming place or imagine themselves as a superhero conquering their fears, they jump right in and create these vivid, detailed worlds. It's like having a built-in movie studio in their heads!

Children are also more suggestible than adults. That critical factor hasn't taken hold yet, so the subconscious is wide open. They're used to listening to adults and taking our word for it (most of the time). So when a trusted adult gives them positive suggestions during hypnosis, like feeling calm and confident, they're more likely to accept and act on those suggestions.

Another great thing about kids is they don't carry around as much emotional baggage as adults do. They haven't spent years worrying about mortgages, jobs, or that embarrassing thing they did in high school. They're more like clean slates, ready to embrace new ideas and positive changes without all the extra mental clutter. Hypnosis can help reinforce good habits, boost their self-esteem, and give them coping tools they'll use for the rest of their life.

They've got the imagination, the suggestibility, and the lack of adult skepticism that make them perfect candidates for hypnosis. One thing to keep in mind however is that since children are so susceptible and enter into hypnosis quickly, use a short induction, and no deepeners. Make it too long and you will lose them to boredom.

A good induction for children would be something like this:

"I wonder if you could close your eyes and try to relax them so much that they wouldn't even open...... close your eyes and see if you can do that....... now pretend that they are just so relaxed they won't open.... Now pretend you're not pretending and test them to see that they are just too relaxed.....stop testing them now and imagine that your whole body can get that relaxed too........ imagine your whole body just relaxing so much that it feels like it went to sleep."

That's all you need to do with a child to get them into the initial state of hypnosis. From there you can start using more of their imagination. With kids, they might be moving and squirming during the hypnosis, but that's fine, it's what they do.

Now there are a lot of things you can use hypnosis for with kids, so you may need to use your own creativity to come up with techniques for their specific issue, but I'll highlight a few of the more common issues that parents can use to create powerful change for their children below. That will be a good starting point for you to come up with your own suggestions. You can also download additional techniques for children by going to my website at mindoverthebody.com and navigating to the children's section.

<u>Technique: The Confidence Superhero Adventure</u>

Step 1: Get Them Comfortable

Find a quiet, comfortable place where your child can sit or lie down without being disturbed. Ensure the environment is comfortable.

Step 2: The Induction

Use the induction above, or simply use a gentle induction technique to help your child relax. This might involve taking deep breaths together or having them imagine a favorite, calming place. Encourage them to close their eyes and take a few deep, calming breaths.

1. **Deep Breathing:** Inhale deeply through the nose, hold for a few seconds, and exhale slowly through the mouth. Repeat this a few times until your child feels calm.
2. **Imagine a Calming Place:** Ask your child to imagine a place where they feel completely safe and happy. This could be a beach, a magical forest, or even their cozy bedroom. Have them visualize the sights, sounds, and smells of this place.

Step 3: Entering the Superhero Adventure

1. **Visualize the Adventure**: Encourage your child to imagine they are about to go on an exciting adventure where they become a confident superhero. They can choose their superhero outfit, powers, and names.
2. **Create the Superhero**: Ask your child to picture themselves as this superhero, feeling strong, brave, and confident. They can imagine what their superhero looks like, the special costume they wear, and the superpowers they have.

Step 4: The Confidence Quest

1. **Start the Adventure**: Have your child imagine they are embarking on a quest to help others and overcome challenges. They can see themselves flying, running, or using their superpowers with ease.
2. **Face Challenges with Confidence**: In their adventure, they encounter different challenges. Maybe there's a tall mountain to climb, a dark forest to navigate, or someone who needs their help. Visualize them tackling each challenge with confidence and success.

Step 5: Celebrating Success

1. **Achieve Victories**: As your child's superhero self overcomes each challenge, they feel more and more confident. Visualize them celebrating each victory with joy and pride.
2. **Receive Applause and Gratitude**: Imagine other characters in the adventure cheering for them and thanking them for their help. This reinforces their sense of accomplishment and confidence.

Step 6: Positive Suggestions for Confidence

While still in the superhero adventure, give your child some positive suggestions to reinforce their confidence. Repeat these affirmations together:

1. "I am a brave and confident superhero."
2. "I can handle any challenge that comes my way."
3. "I believe in myself and my abilities."
4. "I am proud of who I am and what I can do."
5. "I feel strong, brave, and confident every day."

Step 7: Returning to Reality

1. **Return from the Adventure**: Guide your child to imagine returning from their superhero adventure, bringing all the confidence and bravery they felt back with them.

2. **Re-enter the Calming Place:** Have them visualize coming back to their calming place, feeling even more confident and proud of themselves.

Step 8: Returning to Wakefulness

When your child is ready to end the session, have them imagine leaving their calming place, feeling confident and empowered. Count up from one to five together. With each count, encourage your child to feel more alert and energized. By the count of five, have them open their eyes, feeling refreshed and confident.

Technique: Overcome Bullying: The Magic Shield of Confidence

Step 1: Make Them Comfortable

Find a quiet, comfortable place where your child can sit or lie down without being disturbed.

Step 2: Induction

Use the induction above, or use a gentle induction technique to help your child relax. This might involve taking deep breaths together or having them imagine a favorite, calming place. Encourage them to close their eyes and take a few deep, calming breaths.

1. **Deep Breathing:** Inhale deeply through the nose, hold for a few seconds, and exhale slowly through the mouth. Repeat this a few times until your child feels calm.
2. **Imagine a Calming Place:** Ask your child to imagine a place where they feel completely safe and happy. This could be a beach, a magical forest, or even their cozy bedroom. Have them visualize the sights, sounds, and smells of this place.

Step 3: Entering the Safe Place

1. **Visualize the Safe Place:** Encourage your child to picture their special place in as much detail as possible. Remind them that this is a place they can always come back to whenever they need to feel calm and safe.
2. **Anchor the Safe Place:** Let your child know that if they ever feel overwhelmed during this exercise, they can return to this safe place to feel calm and secure again.

Step 4: The Magic Shield of Confidence

1. **Imagine a Magic Shield:** Ask your child to imagine that they have a magic shield of confidence. This shield is beautiful and strong, glowing with a warm, comforting light. It can protect them from any negative words or actions from bullies.
2. **Describe the Shield:** Encourage your child to describe their magic shield in detail. What color is it? Does it have any special designs or symbols on it? How does it feel to hold it?

Step 5: Using the Shield

1. **Visualize the Shield in Action:** Have your child visualize a situation where they might encounter a bully. See them holding their magic shield confidently, with the shield's light protecting them from any hurtful words or actions.
2. **Deflecting Negative Energy:** Imagine the bully's words or actions bouncing off the shield and disappearing. The shield not only protects but also strengthens your child's confidence with each deflected attack.

Step 6: Building Inner Strength

1. **Inner Confidence:** Ask your child to feel the warmth and strength from the shield spreading throughout their body, making them feel more confident and strong.
2. **Positive Inner Voice:** Encourage your child to listen to their positive inner voice, saying things like, "I am strong," "I am brave," and "I am worthy of respect."

Step 7: Positive Suggestions for Confidence

While holding their magic shield, give your child some positive suggestions to reinforce their confidence and resilience. Repeat these affirmations together:

1. "I am protected by my magic shield of confidence."
2. "I am strong and brave, no matter what anyone says."
3. "I believe in myself and my abilities."
4. "I am worthy of respect and kindness."
5. "I can handle any situation with courage and confidence."

Step 8: Returning to Reality

1. **Return from the Visualization:** Guide your child to imagine returning from their visualization, bringing all the confidence and protection from their magic shield with them.
2. **Re-enter the Calming Place:** Have them visualize coming back to their calming place, feeling even more confident and proud of themselves.

Step 9: Returning to Wakefulness

When your child is ready to end the session, have them imagine leaving their calming place, feeling confident and empowered. Count up from one to five together. With each count, encourage your child to feel more alert and energized. By the count of five, have them open their eyes, feeling refreshed and confident.

<u>Technique: The Magical Alarm for Bedwetting</u>

Step 1: Make Your kiddo Comfortable

Find a quiet, comfortable place where your child can sit or lie down without being disturbed.

Step 2: Induction

Use your favorite induction for kids.

Step 3: Entering the Safe Place

1. **Visualize the Safe Place:** Encourage your child to picture their special place in as much detail as possible. Remind them that this is a place they can always come back to whenever they need to feel calm and safe.
2. **Anchor the Safe Place:** Let your child know that if they ever feel overwhelmed during this exercise, they can return to this safe place to feel calm and secure again.

Step 4: Introducing the Magical Alarm

1. **Imagine a Magical Alarm:** Ask your child to imagine that they have a magical alarm inside their body. This alarm is special because it knows exactly when they need to wake up to go to the bathroom.
2. **Describe the Alarm:** Encourage your child to describe their magical alarm. Is it a friendly fairy, a glowing light, or a gentle bell? What color is it? How does it make them feel? How does it wake them up?

Step 5: Activating the Alarm

1. **Visualize the Alarm in Action:** Have your child imagine going to sleep and feeling calm and comfortable. As they drift off, their magical alarm is always on guard, ready to wake them up when it's time to go to the bathroom.
2. **See the Alarm Waking Them Up:** Picture the magical alarm gently waking them up in the middle of the night. They feel a soft nudge or hear a gentle sound, reminding them it's time to go to the bathroom.

Step 6: Practicing the Routine

1. **Going to the Bathroom:** Visualize your child getting out of bed, feeling awake and alert, and walking to the bathroom. They go to the bathroom, feel relieved, and then return to bed, falling back asleep

easily.

2. **Positive Reinforcement:** Imagine this happening smoothly and successfully every night. Each time they wake up and go to the bathroom, they feel proud and confident.

Step 7: Positive Suggestions for Success

While the magical alarm is active, give your child some positive suggestions to reinforce their new routine. Repeat these affirmations together:

1. "My magical alarm helps me wake up when I need to go to the bathroom."
2. "I listen to my body and wake up easily."
3. "I am confident and in control at night."
4. "I can get up, go to the bathroom, and return to sleep easily."
5. "Each night, I wake up and feel proud of myself."

Step 8: Returning to Reality

1. Return from the Visualization: Guide your child to imagine returning from their visualization, bringing all the confidence and control from their magical alarm with them.
2. Re-enter the Calming Place: Have them visualize coming back to their calming place, feeling even more confident and proud of themselves.

Step 9: Returning to Wakefulness

When your child is ready to end the session, have them imagine leaving their calming place, feeling confident and empowered. Count up from one to five together. With each count, encourage your child to feel more alert and energized. By the count of five, have them open their eyes, feeling refreshed and in control.

<u>Technique: The Safe and Loved Bubble For Life Changes</u>

Step 1: Make Them Comfortable

Find a quiet, comfortable place where your child can sit or lie down without being disturbed.

Step 2: Induction

Use your favorite induction or use a gentle technique to help your child relax. Like taking some deep breaths together or having them imagine a favorite, calming place. Encourage them to close their eyes and take a few deep, calming breaths.

1. Deep Breathing: Inhale deeply through the nose, hold for a few seconds, and exhale slowly through the mouth. Repeat this a few times until your child feels calm.
2. Imagine a Calming Place: Ask your child to imagine a place where they feel completely safe and happy. This could be a beach, a magical forest, or even their cozy bedroom. Have them visualize the sights, sounds, and smells of this place.

Step 3: Entering the Safe Place

1. **Visualize the Safe Place**: Encourage your child to picture their special place in as much detail as possible. Remind them that this is a place they can always come back to whenever they need to feel calm and safe.
2. **Anchor the Safe Place**: Let your child know that if they ever feel overwhelmed during this exercise, they can return to this safe place to feel calm and secure again.

Step 4: Creating the Safe and Loved Bubble

1. **Imagine a Bubble of Love**: Ask your child to imagine a beautiful, glowing bubble surrounding them. This bubble is filled with warmth,

love, and safety. It can be any color they like and it sparkles with a magical light.

2. **Describe the Bubble**: Encourage your child to describe their bubble. What color is it? Does it have any special patterns or designs? How does it feel to be inside this bubble?

Step 5: Filling the Bubble with Love and Safety

1. **Visualize Love and Safety**: Have your child imagine that the bubble is filled with all the love and safety in the world. This could be the love from their family, friends, and even their favorite pets.
2. **See the Bubble Glowing**: Picture the bubble glowing brighter and warmer with each loving thought. The bubble protects them from any worries or fears, making them feel completely safe.

Step 6: Taking the Bubble on Adventures

1. **Imagining Life Changes**: Ask your child to imagine a life change they are experiencing, like moving to a new house, starting a new school, or any other change. See them inside their bubble as they face this change.
2. **Feeling Safe During Changes**: Visualize your child going through life change while inside their bubble. They feel safe, loved, and protected no matter what is happening around them.

Step 7: Positive Suggestions for Safety and Love

While in the bubble, give your child some positive suggestions to reinforce their feelings of safety and love. Repeat these affirmations together:

1. "I am safe and loved no matter what changes happen."
2. "My bubble protects me and keeps me feeling happy."
3. "I can handle any change because I am surrounded by love."
4. "I feel calm and secure in my bubble."
5. "I am strong, brave, and always loved."

Step 8: Returning to Reality

1. Return from the Visualization: Guide your child to imagine returning from their visualization, bringing all the safety and love from their bubble with them.
2. Re-enter the Calming Place: Have them visualize coming back to their calming place, feeling even more confident and loved.

Step 9: Returning to Wakefulness

When your child is ready to end the session, have them imagine leaving their calming place, feeling safe and loved. Count up from one to five together. With each count, encourage your child to feel more alert and energized. By the count of five, have them open their eyes, feeling refreshed and secure.

Technique: Helping Kids with Autism-the Comfort Creature

Autism comes with its own set of challenges, but also unique strengths. Hypnosis can be a fantastic tool to help kids on the spectrum manage anxiety, improve focus, enhance social skills, handle sensory overload, build self-esteem, and communicate better. By tapping into the power of their imagination and subconscious mind, hypnosis gives kids practical tools to navigate their world with more ease and confidence.

Kids with autism experience the world in their own unique way. They might find some everyday situations challenging, but they also have special abilities that make them stand out. While hypnosis isn't a magic cure, it can definitely help kids manage some of the difficulties they face and make the most of their strengths.

Step 1: Make Yourself Comfortable

Find a quiet, comfortable place where you and your child can sit or lie down without being disturbed. Ensure the environment is welcoming and free of distractions.

Step 2: Induction

Use a gentle induction technique to help your child enter a relaxed state. This might involve deep breathing, listening to calming music, or imagining a peaceful place. Allow them to relax deeply and completely.

Step 3: Entering the Visualization

1. **Imagine a Safe and Magical Garden**: Picture yourselves entering a safe and magical garden. This garden is filled with colorful flowers, friendly animals, and gentle sounds of nature. Visualize the sights, sounds, and feelings of this place, and let your child fully immerse in its calming and supportive energy.
2. **Describe the Garden**: Think about the details of the garden. Are there butterflies, a gentle stream, and the soft rustling of leaves? How does it feel to be in this place of tranquility and wonder?

Step 4: Visualizing a Comfort Creature

1. **Visualize a Comfort Creature**: Imagine meeting a friendly, magical creature in the garden. This creature is here to provide comfort, support, and understanding. It could be a gentle dragon, a wise owl, or a playful dolphin. See the creature clearly in your mind and notice its unique details.
2. **Describe the Creature**: Think about how this creature looks and feels. Is it soft and cuddly, with big, kind eyes? How does it feel to be with this Comfort Creature?

Step 5: Building a Connection with the Creature

1. **Visualize Interacting with the Creature**: Imagine your child interacting with the Comfort Creature. They might be petting it, talking to it, or simply sitting together. Feel the connection and trust building between them.

2. **Feel the Comfort**: As your child spends time with the Comfort Creature, feel its calming and supportive energy spreading through their body. Imagine the creature helping your child feel safe, understood, and loved.

Step 6: Using the Creature's Support

1. **Visualize the Creature Offering Help**: Imagine the Comfort Creature offering its help in different situations. It might give your child advice, offer a comforting presence, or provide a special gift like a calming stone or a magical shield.
2. **Feel the Support**: As the creature offers its help, feel the sense of support and confidence growing within your child. Imagine them using this support in their daily life, whether it's during school, at home, or with friends.

Step 7: Positive Suggestions for Managing Challenges

While in the magical garden, give your child some positive suggestions to reinforce their ability to manage challenges and feel confident. Repeat these affirmations together:

1. "I am strong and capable."
2. "I can handle any challenge with calm and confidence."
3. "I am loved and supported."
4. "I have a special friend to help me whenever I need it."
5. "I am proud of who I am."

Step 8: Embracing the Supportive State

1. **Visualize Embracing the Creature**: Imagine your child embracing the Comfort Creature with gratitude and appreciation. Visualize them feeling supported, confident, and understood in various situations, whether it's learning new things, playing, or interacting with others.

2. **Feel the Empowerment**: As your child embraces this supportive state, feel a sense of empowerment and confidence. Know that they have the ability to manage and overcome their challenges.

Step 9: Returning to Reality

1. **Return from the Visualization**: Imagine gradually returning from your visualization, bringing all the comfort and support from the exercise with you. See yourselves leaving the magical garden but knowing the benefits stay with you.
2. **Re-enter the Calming Place**: Visualize coming back to your calming place, feeling even more determined and ready to use the support and confidence gained from the Comfort Creature.

Step 10: Returning to Wakefulness

When you are ready to end the session, imagine leaving your calming place, feeling refreshed and empowered. Count up from one to five. With each count, feel yourselves becoming more alert and ready to engage in the day. By the count of five, open your eyes, feeling refreshed and in control.

Chapter 19: Dealing with Grief

Loss is a part of life. Whether it's the loss of a loved one, the end of a significant relationship, or other major life changes. That loss often comes with a period of grief. Grief is something that is natural, and understandable, but when we stay in a state of grief for too long, it often becomes a problem preventing us from moving forward and living our most fulfilling lives. In these extended periods of grief, it becomes less about the loss we experienced and more about us feeling sorry for ourselves and not living our lives to the fullest.

If we are grieving over the loss of a loved one, we lose sight of the fact that they wouldn't want us not to make the most of our lives because they are no longer here with us. I'm sure they would rather have us focused on good past memories and gratitude for the time you did have together. I'll offer a technique to help you focus on gratitude rather than grief when dealing with the loss of a loved one.

Another thing people tend to grieve over is the loss of a significant relationship. Losing a significant relationship is hard. It can feel like having your heart ripped out and trying to figure out how to move forward. You're not just mourning the person, but all the plans and dreams you shared. It's normal to feel a mix of sadness, anger, and confusion, and sometimes it can feel like a huge void in your life. Grieving isn't just about the end of the relationship; it's also about finding yourself again and rebuilding your hope and plans for the future.

And then there is grief over major life changes. Major life changes can bring on a lot of emotions, and it's completely normal to feel overwhelmed by it all. Whether it's moving to a new city, losing a job, or dealing with a big shift in your personal life, these changes can feel like you're losing a part of yourself.

It's okay to feel sad, anxious, or even scared about what's next. You'll find your footing again and start to see the new opportunities that come with change. Through self-hypnosis, you can be more open to those hidden opportunities and more accepting of the change.

Technique: Healing Heart Visualization for Grief

Step 1: Make Yourself Comfortable

Find a quiet, comfortable place where you can sit or lie down without being disturbed. Ensure the environment is cozy and welcoming.

Step 2: Induction and Deepening

Use your favorite induction and deepening technique.

Step 3: Entering the Safe Place

1. **Visualize the Safe Place**: Imagine yourself in this special place, feeling safe and at ease. Remind yourself that you can return to this place whenever you need to feel calm and secure.
2. **Anchor the Safe Place**: Know that if your emotions become too intense during this exercise, you can return to this safe place to regain your calm.

Step 4: Connecting with Your Loved One

1. **Imagine a Healing Light**: Visualize a warm, glowing light surrounding you. This light represents love, comfort, and healing. Feel its warmth and let it soothe you.
2. **Visualize Your Loved One**: Picture your loved one in this light. See them looking peaceful and happy, radiating love towards you.

Step 5: Expressing Your Emotions

1. **Talk to Your Loved One**: In your mind, have a conversation with your loved one. Express your feelings of grief, sadness, and loss. Tell them how much you miss them and share any thoughts or emotions

you need to let out.

2. **Listen to Their Response:** Imagine your loved one responding with words of comfort and love. Hear them reassure you that it's okay and that they are at peace. Listen as they tell you to focus on their life, not their passing.

Step 6: Healing Your Heart

1. **Visualize a Healing Heart:** Imagine your heart being gently surrounded by the warm, glowing light. See this light healing the cracks and wounds left by your loss.
2. **Fill Your Heart with Love:** Visualize your heart filling up with love, both from your loved one and from your own reservoir of love and memories. Feel this love strengthening and comforting you.

Step 7: Positive Suggestions for Healing

While your heart is filled with healing light, give yourself some positive suggestions to reinforce your healing process. Repeat these affirmations to yourself:

1. "I am surrounded by love and healing."
2. "I can focus on the gratitude for for time we had together"
3. "My loved one's love continues to support and comfort me."
4. "I carry my loved one's memory with me, which brings me strength."
5. "Each day, I find more peace and healing in my heart."

Step 8: Returning to Reality

1. **Return from the Visualization:** Imagine gradually returning from your visualization, bringing all the love and healing from the exercise with you.
2. **Re-enter the Calming Place:** Visualize coming back to your calming place, feeling even more peaceful and comforted.

Step 9: Returning to Wakefulness

When you are ready to end the session, imagine leaving your calming place, feeling healed and loved. Count up from one to five. With each count, feel yourself becoming more alert and energized. By the count of five, open your eyes, feeling refreshed and comforted.

Technique: Rebuilding Your Heart After a Breakup

Step 1: Make Yourself Comfortable

Find a quiet, comfortable place where you can sit or lie down without being disturbed.
Step 2: Induction and Deepening
Use your favorite induction and deepener.

Step 3: Entering the Safe Place

1. **Visualize the Safe Place:** Imagine yourself in a special place, feeling safe and at ease. Remind yourself that you can return to this place whenever you need to feel calm and secure.

Step 4: Acknowledging the Loss

1. **Reflect on the Relationship:** Picture the significant relationship that has ended. Acknowledge the emotions you feel about this loss, whether it's sadness, anger, confusion, or relief. Allow yourself to feel these emotions without judgment.
2. **Visualize a Box:** Imagine a beautiful, strong box in front of you. This box is for holding your memories and emotions related to the relationship.

Step 5: Placing Emotions in the Box

1. **Identify Your Emotions:** Think about the different emotions you're experiencing and visualize them as tangible objects. For example, sadness might be a blue orb, anger a red flame, and confusion a swirling mist.
2. **Place Them in the Box:** One by one, place these objects into the box. As you do, acknowledge each emotion, thank it for its role in your

healing, and let it go.

Step 6: Visualizing a Healing Light

1. **Imagine a Healing Light**: Visualize a warm, glowing light surrounding you. This light represents love, comfort, and healing. Feel its warmth and let it soothe you.
2. **See the Light Filling Your Heart**: Imagine the healing light filling your heart, mending the cracks and wounds left by the end of the relationship. Feel the light bringing you peace and strength.

Step 7: Rebuilding Your Heart

1. **Create a New Vision:** Visualize your heart as a beautiful, strong structure. Imagine rebuilding it with the lessons and growth you've gained from the relationship.
2. **Fill Your Heart with Positive Energy:** Picture your heart filling with positive energy, self-love, and hope for the future. See yourself becoming stronger and more resilient.

Step 8: Positive Suggestions for Moving Forward

While your heart is filled with healing light, give yourself some positive suggestions to reinforce your healing process. Repeat these affirmations to yourself:

1. "I am healing and growing stronger every day."
2. "It's okay to feel sad and take my time to heal."
3. "I carry the lessons from this relationship with me and use them to grow."
4. "I am worthy of love, and I love myself deeply."
5. "Each day, I move forward with hope and confidence."

Step 9: Returning to Reality

1. **Return from the Visualization:** Imagine gradually returning from your visualization, bringing all the healing and positive energy from the exercise with you.
2. **Re-enter the Calming Place:** Visualize coming back to your calming place, feeling even more peaceful and comforted.

Step 10: Returning to Wakefulness

When you are ready to end the session, imagine leaving your calming place, feeling healed and empowered. Count up from one to five. With each count, feel yourself becoming more alert and energized. By the count of five, open your eyes, feeling refreshed and confident.

<u>Technique: Embracing Life Changes with Serenity</u>

Step 1: Make Yourself Comfortable

Find a quiet, comfortable place where you can sit or lie down without being disturbed.

Step 2: Induction and Deepening

Use a gentle induction technique to help yourself relax. Close your eyes and begin to breathe deeply, letting go of any tension in your body.

Step 3: Visualizing the Safe Haven

1. **Imagine a Safe Haven:** Picture yourself in a safe, serene place where you feel completely at ease. This could be a quiet beach, a tranquil forest, or a cozy room. Visualize the sights, sounds, and smells of this place, and let yourself fully immerse in its peacefulness.

Step 4: Embracing the Life Change

1. **Visualize the Life Change:** Bring to mind the life change you are grieving. This could be moving to a new city, changing jobs, or any other significant transition. See this change as a path or journey in front of you.
2. **Step onto the Path:** Imagine yourself stepping onto this path, feeling a mix of emotions. Acknowledge these feelings without judgment, allowing them to be present.

Step 5: Finding Strength and Comfort

1. **Visualize a Guiding Light:** Picture a warm, guiding light above you. This light represents strength, comfort, and guidance. Feel its warmth surrounding you, giving you the courage to face life change.
2. **See the Light Filling You:** Imagine the guiding light filling your

body with peace and strength. As it does, see any fears or worries melting away, replaced by a sense of calm and confidence.

Step 6: Embracing the Journey

1. **Visualize Positive Outcomes:** Picture positive outcomes and opportunities arising from this life change. See yourself adapting and thriving in this new situation. Visualize yourself meeting new people, discovering new passions, or finding new strengths.
2. **Feel the Support:** Imagine feeling supported by the people who care about you. Visualize their encouragement and love surrounding you, helping you navigate this change.

Step 7: Positive Suggestions for Embracing Change

While immersed in this peaceful visualization, give yourself some positive suggestions to reinforce your acceptance and adaptation to life change. Repeat these affirmations to yourself:

1. "I am strong and capable of handling this change."
2. "I embrace new opportunities with confidence and hope."
3. "I am supported and loved as I navigate this transition."
4. "I trust in my ability to adapt and thrive."
5. "Each day, I move forward with peace and confidence."

Step 8: Returning to Reality

1. **Return from the Visualization:** Imagine gradually returning from your visualization, bringing all the peace and positive energy from the exercise with you. See yourself stepping off the path and back into your safe haven.
2. **Re-enter the Calming Place:** Visualize coming back to your calming place, feeling even more serene and confident.

Step 9: Returning to Wakefulness

When you are ready to end the session, imagine leaving your calming place, feeling empowered and at peace. Count up from one to five. With each count, feel yourself becoming more alert and energized. By the count of five, open your eyes, feeling refreshed and ready to embrace the changes in your life.

Chapter 20: Chronic Pain and Physical Healing

In this section, we will look at dealing with chronic pain as well as healing faster from surgery or physical injury.

It's been proven time and time again that hypnosis can be one of the most effective ways to help people manage, and in some cases, completely remove chronic pain. No one experiencing pain wants to hear "It's all in your head", but the reality is that all pain is created in the mind, we just experience it in the body.

Now before we get too deep, it's important to understand that pain serves a purpose and you should always have the source of any pain diagnosed. Pain is a warning signal that something isn't right and needs to be addressed. With my individual clients, I always make sure that pain has been diagnosed and that removing that pain won't cause any possibility of additional injury or damage, and in some cases require a referral from the doctor treating the source of that pain. If however your pain has been diagnosed and reducing or eliminating that pain won't cause any negative consequences, there really isn't any reason to live with it any longer.

Pain is nothing more than neurotransmitters from the body being sent to the brain to alert it of a problem. The actual sensation of pain is created by the mind to let you know what the body just told it. It's the mind's only way to make sure you are aware of it, and that you don't overuse the area or help protect it.

Through hypnosis, you can instruct the mind to do something else with that signal or turn it off completely. You can get relief that is more effective than pain medications and that power is something you already have available to you. If Western medicine practitioners would use people's own ability to reduce or eliminate pain, the need to prescribe addictive narcotics would be a fraction of what it is today.

Chronic pain is often more than just physical discomfort, there's often an emotional side to it as well. It's not just about the aching muscles or sore joints—our feelings and mental state play a huge role. When we're stressed, anxious, or dealing with unresolved trauma, it can make our bodies tense up, leading to chronic pain. For example, someone with a lot of stress might end up with chronic back pain because their muscles are always tight.

This connection between emotions and pain can create a nasty cycle. Pain can make us feel stressed or depressed, and those emotions can actually make the pain worse. Think about it, if you're feeling hopeless or constantly worried about your pain, it can feel even more intense. This is because stress and anxiety trigger the body's stress response, releasing hormones that can amplify pain signals. Plus, dealing with chronic pain often means dealing with a lot of loss—like not being able to do the things you used to enjoy—which can lead to feelings of grief and sadness, making the pain feel even worse.

To really tackle chronic pain, it's important to address both the physical and emotional aspects. That's where hypnosis can play a big part in resolving the pain. Hypnosis can help you process and let go of negative emotions, which can, in turn, help reduce your pain. Realizing that your pain has an emotional component can be empowering because it means there are more ways to find relief. By working on both your mind and body, you can start to break the cycle of pain and emotional distress and get back to living your life.

When someone is reluctant to accept that all pain is created in the mind, and can be resolved there as well, I usually ask them to explain how someone who has lost a limb can still feel pain. The part of the body no longer exists, but the pain and sensations are still there. Even though the limb is no longer there, the brain can still send and receive pain signals from the nerves that used to be connected to the missing limb. The brain hasn't fully adjusted to the new reality of the missing limb and continues to produce sensations as if the limb were still there. This can lead to some pretty intense and sometimes distressing sensations for those who experience it.

Understanding that all pain and physical sensations are created in the mind opens up new ways to manage and treat pain. If the brain can create pain, it can also be trained to manage, reduce, or eliminate it. Hypnosis can help rewire the brain's response to pain. By changing the way we think about and interpret pain, we can actually change our physical experience of it. My goal is to give you more control over your pain and help you find new ways to live more comfortably.

It's not just pain that can be improved with hypnosis, even physical injuries such as broken bones and post-surgery healing can be accelerated. Some studies have shown that using hypnosis during recovery from surgery or injury can be up to 41% faster than people who rely solely on Western medicine.

Let's take a look at some techniques that I've used successfully in helping people overcome pain and increase the body's natural healing ability, but also remember, if there is an emotional connection to that pain, use the other techniques to resolve that as well.

Technique: Removing Chronic Pain Through Dissociation

This technique is based on having the mind see the pain as something that is dissociated from you. Something that isn't part of you and that can be removed and sent away.

Step 1: Make Yourself Comfortable

Find a quiet, comfortable place where you can sit or lie down without being disturbed. Ensure the environment is free of distractions.

Step 2: Induction and Deepening

Use your favorite induction and deepening technique to enter a relaxed state. When pain or discomfort is present it is usually best to use a more rapid induction.

Step 3: Entering the Visualization

1. **Imagine a Safe, Calming Place**: Picture yourself in a safe, serene environment where you feel completely relaxed and at peace. This could be a tranquil beach, a cozy room, or a lush forest. Visualize the sights, sounds, and feelings of this place, and let yourself fully immerse in its calming and protective energy.
2. **Describe the Environment**: Think about the details of this place. Are there gentle waves, soft lighting, or birds singing? How does it feel to be in this place of comfort and tranquility?

Step 4: Identifying the Pain

1. **Visualize the Pain**: Imagine the chronic pain you experience as a tangible object within your body. It could be a dark cloud, a heavy weight, or a tight knot. See this object clearly and focus on its presence.

2. **Describe the Pain**: Think about how this object looks and feels. Is it dense, sharp, or throbbing? How does it affect your body and your sense of well-being?

Step 5: Dissociating from the Pain

1. **Visualize Removing the Pain**: Imagine reaching into your body and gently removing the object representing your pain. See yourself pulling it out, feeling lighter and more relieved as it leaves your body.
2. **Feel the Release**: As you remove the pain, feel a sense of release and relief. Imagine the pain no longer being a part of you, but something external that you can control.

Step 6: Attaching the Pain to a Balloon

1. **Visualize a Balloon**: Picture a large, colorful helium balloon floating beside you. This balloon represents freedom and release.
2. **Tie the Pain to the Balloon**: Imagine tying the object of your pain securely to the balloon. See the pain attached to the balloon, ready to be carried away.

Step 7: Releasing the Balloon

1. **Visualize Releasing the Balloon**: Imagine letting go of the balloon and watching it rise into the sky. See it lifting higher and higher, taking the pain with it. As the balloon ascends, the pain becomes smaller and more distant until it finally disappears.
2. **Feel the Freedom**: As you watch the balloon and pain disappear, feel a deep sense of freedom and relief. Know that the pain is no longer part of you, and you are free from its grasp.

Step 8: Positive Suggestions for Pain-Free Living

While in your calming place, give yourself some positive suggestions to reinforce your commitment to living without pain. Repeat these affirmations to yourself:

1. "I am free from chronic pain."
2. "My body is relaxed and comfortable."
3. "I release all pain and embrace a life of ease."
4. "I am in control of my body and my well-being."
5. "Each day, I feel healthier and stronger."

Step 9: Embracing the Pain-Free State

1. **Visualize Embracing Your Health**: Imagine embracing your body with gratitude and appreciation. Visualize yourself living a pain-free life, engaging in activities you love, and feeling vibrant and energetic.
2. **Feel the Empowerment**: As you embrace this new state, feel a sense of empowerment and confidence. Know that you have the ability to manage and overcome chronic pain.

Step 10: Returning to Reality

1. **Return from the Visualization**: Imagine gradually returning from your visualization, bringing all the relief and positivity from the exercise with you. See yourself leaving the calming place but knowing the benefits stay with you.
2. **Re-enter the Calming Place**: Visualize coming back to your calming place, feeling even more determined and ready to live a pain-free life.

Step 11: Returning to Wakefulness

When you are ready to end the session, imagine leaving your calming place, feeling refreshed and empowered. Count up from one to five. With each count, feel yourself becoming more alert and ready to engage in your day. By the count of five, open your eyes, feeling refreshed and in control.

Technique: Removing Chronic Pain with the Pain Blocking Gate Technique

In this technique, we create a mental barrier that blocks the pain signal coming from the body. I have had great results with this type of technique for chronic pain.

Step 1: Make Yourself Comfortable

Find a quiet, comfortable place where you can sit or lie down without being disturbed. Ensure the environment is free of distractions.

Step 2: Induction and Deepening

Use your favorite induction and deepening technique to enter a relaxed state. For chronic pain, it is usually best to use a rapid induction rather than a slower progressive relaxation induction.

Step 3: Entering the Visualization

1. **Imagine a Tranquil Path**: Picture yourself walking along a tranquil path that leads to a beautiful garden. This garden is filled with vibrant flowers, lush greenery, and the gentle sounds of nature. Visualize the sights, sounds, and feelings of this place, and let yourself fully immerse in its calming and rejuvenating energy.
2. **Describe the Garden**: Think about the details of the garden. Are there colorful flowers, a gentle stream, and birds singing? How does it feel to be in this place of peace and healing?

Step 4: Visualizing the Pain Gate

1. **Visualize the Pain Gate**: As you walk through the garden, imagine coming across a large gate. This gate represents the barrier between your chronic pain and your body's ability to feel relief. The gate has

the ability to block or allow the passage of pain signals.

2. **Describe the Gate**: Think about how this gate looks and feels. Is it made of strong, solid material? Does it have a lock or a control panel? How does it feel to stand before this gate?

Step 5: Identifying the Pain

1. **Visualize the Pain**: Imagine the chronic pain you experience as a stream of dark, heavy particles flowing towards the gate. See this stream clearly and focus on its presence.
2. **Describe the Pain**: Think about how these particles look and feel. Are they dense, sharp, or throbbing? How does it feel to visualize these particles approaching the gate?

Step 6: Closing the Pain Gate

1. **Visualize Closing the Gate**: Imagine yourself walking up to the gate and taking control of it. Visualize yourself using a key, turning a dial, or pressing a button to close the gate. As you do, see the gate slowly closing and blocking the stream of pain particles from passing through.
2. **Feel the Relief**: As the gate closes, feel a sense of relief and comfort spreading throughout your body. Imagine the pain being blocked by the gate, unable to reach you and affect you anymore.

Step 7: Reinforcing the Gate

1. **Visualize Reinforcing the Gate**: Imagine adding extra locks, bolts, or layers of protection to the gate, making it even stronger and more secure. See the gate becoming impenetrable, ensuring that the pain cannot pass through.
2. **Feel the Security**: As you reinforce the gate, feel a deep sense of security and confidence. Know that the gate is strong and will protect you from the pain.

Step 8: Positive Suggestions for Pain-Free Living

While in your beautiful garden, give yourself some positive suggestions to reinforce your commitment to living without pain. Repeat these affirmations to yourself:

1. "My body is protected from pain."
2. "I am in control of my pain and my body."
3. "I feel relaxed and comfortable."
4. "I live a life free from chronic pain."
5. "Each day, I become healthier and stronger."

Step 9: Embracing the Pain-Free State

1. **Visualize Embracing Your Health**: Imagine embracing your body with gratitude and appreciation. Visualize yourself living a pain-free life, engaging in activities you love, and feeling vibrant and energetic.
2. **Feel the Empowerment**: As you embrace this new state, feel a sense of empowerment and confidence. Know that you have the ability to manage and overcome chronic pain.

Step 10: Returning to Reality

1. **Return from the Visualization**: Imagine gradually returning from your visualization, bringing all the relief and positivity from the exercise with you. See yourself leaving the beautiful garden but knowing the benefits stay with you.
2. **Re-enter the Calming Place**: Visualize coming back to your calming place, feeling even more determined and ready to live a pain-free life.

Step 11: Returning to Wakefulness

When you are ready to end the session, imagine leaving your calming place, feeling refreshed and empowered. Count up from one to five. With each count, feel yourself becoming more alert and ready to engage in your day. By the count of five, open your eyes, feeling refreshed and in control.

Technique: Removing Pain With Complete Relaxation

For pain that has muscular tension as one of the main issues, sometimes all we need to do is release that tension and relax the mind and body as much as possible.

Step 1: Make Yourself Comfortable

Find a quiet, comfortable place where you can sit or lie down without being disturbed. Ensure the environment is free of distractions.

Step 2: Induction and Deepening

Use your favorite induction and deepening technique to enter a relaxed state. This might involve deep breathing, progressive muscle relaxation, or imagining a peaceful place. Allow yourself to relax deeply and completely.

Step 3: Entering the Visualization

1. **Imagine a Calming Room**: Picture yourself entering a beautifully calming room. This room is designed for relaxation and healing, filled with soft lighting, comfortable seating, and a tranquil atmosphere. Visualize the sights, sounds, and feelings of this place, and let yourself fully immerse in its calming energy.
2. **Describe the Room**: Think about the details of the room. Are there soft cushions, gentle music, or the scent of calming essential oils? How does it feel to be in this place of comfort and peace?

Step 4: Identifying the Pain Area

1. **Focus on the Pain Area**: Bring your attention to the area of your body where you experience pain. Visualize this area clearly and focus on its sensations. Notice any tension, tightness, or discomfort.
2. **Describe the Pain**: Think about how this area looks and feels. Is it

tense, throbbing, or sore? How does it affect your overall sense of well-being?

Step 5: Visualizing Relaxation

1. **Visualize the Pain Area Relaxing**: Imagine a warm, soothing light enveloping the area of pain. See this light gently penetrating your skin and muscles, bringing a deep sense of relaxation and comfort. Visualize the muscles in this area loosening and the tension melting away.
2. **Feel the Relaxation**: As the light continues to soothe the pain area, feel a wave of relaxation spreading through your body. Imagine the pain dissipating and being replaced by a sense of calm and ease.

Step 6: Enhancing the Relaxation

1. **Visualize Breathing into the Pain Area**: Imagine breathing deeply and directing your breath into the area of pain. With each inhale, bring in more of the soothing light, and with each exhale, release any remaining tension and discomfort.
2. **Feel the Release**: As you breathe into the pain area, feel the relaxation deepening. Imagine the pain being carried away with each exhale, leaving the area completely relaxed and pain-free.

Step 7: Positive Suggestions for Pain-Free Living

While in your calming room, give yourself some positive suggestions to reinforce your commitment to living without pain. Repeat these affirmations to yourself:

1. "My body is relaxed and comfortable."
2. "I release all pain and tension."
3. "I am in control of my body's well-being."
4. "Each breath brings me comfort and relief."
5. "I live a life free from pain and full of ease."

Step 8: Embracing the Pain-Free State

1. **Visualize Embracing Your Health**: Imagine embracing your body with gratitude and appreciation. Visualize yourself living a pain-free life, engaging in activities you love, and feeling vibrant and energetic.
2. **Feel the Empowerment**: As you embrace this new state, feel a sense of empowerment and confidence. Know that you have the ability to manage and overcome chronic pain.

Step 9: Returning to Reality

1. **Return from the Visualization**: Imagine gradually returning from your visualization, bringing all the relief and positivity from the exercise with you. See yourself leaving the calming room but knowing the benefits stay with you.
2. **Re-enter the Calming Place**: Visualize coming back to your calming place, feeling even more determined and ready to live a pain-free life.

Step 10: Returning to Wakefulness

When you are ready to end the session, imagine leaving your calming place, feeling refreshed and empowered. Count up from one to five. With each count, feel yourself becoming more alert and ready to engage in your day. By the count of five, open your eyes, feeling refreshed and in control.

Technique: Removing Migraine Pain by Visualizing Blood Vessels Expanding

This technique can help overcome migraine pain quickly. If you suffer from migraines, make sure that you have had a diagnosis to ensure there is no serious underlying condition that needs to be addressed.

Step 1: Make Yourself Comfortable

Find a quiet, comfortable place where you can sit or lie down without being disturbed. Ensure the environment is free of distractions.

Step 2: Induction and Deepening

Use your favorite induction and deepening technique to enter a relaxed state.

Step 3: Entering the Visualization

1. **Imagine Floating in a Soothing Ocean**: Picture yourself floating effortlessly in a warm, soothing ocean under a clear blue sky. The water is calm and gentle, and it supports your body completely, allowing you to float with ease. Visualize the sights, sounds, and feelings of this place, and let yourself fully immerse in its calming and rejuvenating energy.
2. **Describe the Ocean**: Think about the details of the ocean. Are there gentle waves lapping around you, the soft glow of the sun warming your skin, and the distant calls of seabirds? How does it feel to be in this place of tranquility and weightlessness?

Step 4: Focusing on the Migraine

1. **Identify the Pain Area**: Bring your attention to the area of your head where you feel the migraine. Visualize this area clearly and focus on its sensations. Notice any tightness, throbbing, or pressure.
2. **Describe the Pain**: Think about how this area looks and feels. Is it

tense, pulsating, or aching? How does it affect your overall sense of well-being?

Step 5: Visualizing Blood Vessels Expanding

1. **Visualize the Blood Vessels**: Imagine the blood vessels in your head. See them clearly as tubes or channels that might be constricted or narrow due to the migraine.
2. **Describe the Blood Vessels**: Think about how these blood vessels look and feel. Are they tight, narrow, or throbbing? How does it feel to focus on these blood vessels?

Step 6: Expanding the Blood Vessels

1. **Visualize Expanding the Vessels**: Imagine a warm, soothing light emanating from the sun above, penetrating the water and surrounding your head. See this light gently penetrating the blood vessels, causing them to relax and expand. Visualize the vessels widening and allowing blood to flow more freely.
2. **Feel the Relief**: As the blood vessels expand, feel a wave of relief spreading through your head. Imagine the pressure and pain dissipating as the vessels continue to widen and relax.

Step 7: Enhancing the Relaxation

1. **Visualize Breathing into the Pain Area**: Imagine breathing deeply and directing your breath into the area of pain. With each inhale, bring in more of the soothing light, and with each exhale, release any remaining tension and discomfort.
2. **Feel the Release**: As you breathe into the pain area, feel the relaxation deepening. Imagine the pain being carried away with each exhale, leaving the area completely relaxed and pain-free.

Step 8: Positive Suggestions for Pain-Free Living

While floating in the soothing ocean, give yourself some positive suggestions to reinforce your commitment to living without migraines. Repeat these affirmations to yourself:

1. "My blood vessels are relaxed and open."
2. "I release all tension and pain."
3. "I am in control of my body's well-being."
4. "Each breath brings me comfort and relief."
5. "I live a life free from migraines and full of ease."

Step 9: Embracing the Pain-Free State

1. **Visualize Embracing Your Health**: Imagine embracing your body with gratitude and appreciation. Visualize yourself living a pain-free life, engaging in activities you love, and feeling vibrant and energetic.
2. **Feel the Empowerment**: As you embrace this new state, feel a sense of empowerment and confidence. Know that you have the ability to manage and overcome migraines.

Step 10: Returning to Reality

1. **Return from the Visualization**: Imagine gradually returning from your visualization, bringing all the relief and positivity from the exercise with you. See yourself leaving the soothing ocean but knowing the benefits stay with you.
2. **Re-enter the Calming Place**: Visualize coming back to your calming place, feeling even more determined and ready to live a migraine-free life.

Step 11: Returning to Wakefulness

When you are ready to end the session, imagine leaving your calming place, feeling refreshed and empowered. Count up from one to five. With each count, feel yourself becoming more alert and ready to engage in your day. By the count of five, open your eyes, feeling refreshed and in control.

Technique: The Glove of Anesthesia

This technique is to create complete numbness in an area of the body. It's like hypno-novocaine. This technique is not a long-term solution but can be extremely helpful prior to a medical procedure or a trip to the dentist. It is also a great technique for those who have an issue with needles. Done correctly, you will create numbness in your hand and transfer that numbness to any area of the body.

Step 1: Make Yourself Comfortable

Find a quiet, comfortable place where you can sit or lie down without being disturbed. Ensure the environment is free of distractions.

Step 2: Induction and Deepening

Use your favorite induction and deepening technique to enter a relaxed state. This technique requires a deeper level of trance, so deepen your trance as much as possible.

Step 3: Entering the Visualization

1. **Imagine a Calm, Healing Space**: Picture yourself in a calm, healing space. This could be a cozy room, a tranquil beach, or a lush forest. Visualize the sights, sounds, and feelings of this place, and let yourself fully immerse in its soothing energy.
2. **Describe the Space**: Think about the details of this space. Are there gentle waves, soft lighting, or the scent of calming essential oils? How does it feel to be in this place of relaxation and healing?

Step 4: Visualizing the Bucket of Ice Water

1. **Visualize a Bucket of Ice Water**: Imagine a bucket filled with freezing cold water and ice. This water is so cold that it can numb

anything it touches. See the bucket clearly in your mind and notice the frosty condensation on its sides.

2. **Describe the Bucket**: Think about how this bucket looks and feels. Is it made of metal, with ice cubes floating in the water? Make it look as cold as possible.

Step 5: Placing Your Hand in the Ice Water

1. **Visualize Placing Your Hand in the Water**: Imagine gently and slowly placing your hand into the bucket of ice water. As your hand touches the freezing water, feel the coldness enveloping your hand and spreading through your fingers and palms.

2. **Feel the Numbness in Your Hand**: As your hand stays in the water, feel it becoming numb and losing all sensation. The coldness penetrates deeply, creating a complete lack of sensation in your hand.

Step 6: Transferring the Anesthesia

1. **Visualize Removing Your Hand**: Imagine taking your now numb hand out of the bucket of ice water. Feel the numbness and lack of sensation in your hand.

2. **Visualize Touching the Painful Area**: Imagine gently placing your numb hand on the area of your body where you feel pain. As you touch this area, visualize the numbness and anesthesia transferring from your hand to the painful spot. It can be helpful to see the numbness as a color as well, see that color and numbness transfer to the area needing the anesthesia.

Step 7: Feeling the Numbness Spread

1. **Visualize the Numbness Spreading**: As the anesthesia transfers, feel the cold, tingling sensation spreading through the painful area. Imagine the pain fading away, replaced by a deep sense of numbness and comfort.

2. **Feel the Relief**: As the numbness spreads, feel a profound sense of relief and comfort. Know that you are in control of your body's sensations and that you can create numbness and relief whenever you need it.

Step 8: Positive Suggestions for Pain-Free Living

While in your calm, healing space, give yourself some positive suggestions to reinforce your commitment to living without pain. Repeat these affirmations to yourself:

1. "I am in control of my body's sensations."
2. "I can create numbness and comfort whenever I need it."
3. "I release all pain and embrace a life of ease."
4. "Each breath brings me comfort and relief."
5. "I live a life free from pain and full of peace."

Step 9: Embracing the Pain-Free State

1. **Visualize Embracing Your Health**: Imagine embracing your body with gratitude and appreciation. Visualize yourself living a pain-free life, engaging in activities you love, and feeling vibrant and energetic.
2. **Feel the Empowerment**: As you embrace this new state, feel a sense of empowerment and confidence. Know that you have the ability to manage and overcome pain.

Step 10: Returning to Reality

1. **Return from the Visualization**: Imagine gradually returning from your visualization, bringing all the relief and positivity from the exercise with you. See yourself leaving the calm, healing space but knowing the benefits stay with you.
2. **Re-enter the Calming Place**: Visualize coming back to your calming place, feeling even more determined and ready to live a pain-free life.

Step 11: Returning to Wakefulness

When you are ready to end the session, imagine leaving your calming place, feeling refreshed and empowered. Count up from one to five. With each count, feel yourself becoming more alert and ready to engage in your day. By the count of five, open your eyes, feeling refreshed and in control.

Technique: Accelerating Healing from Surgery or Physical Injury

This technique is for accelerating healing after a physical injury or surgery. Your mind is in charge of the resources it sends to any injured area, and by directing it you can accelerate that healing by up to 41% faster.

Step 1: Make Yourself Comfortable

Find a quiet, comfortable place where you can sit or lie down without being disturbed. Ensure the environment is free of distractions.

Step 2: Induction and Deepening

Use your favorite induction and deepening technique to enter a relaxed state. This might involve deep breathing, progressive muscle relaxation, or imagining a peaceful place. Allow yourself to relax deeply and completely.

Step 3: Entering the Visualization

1. **Imagine a Healing Ocean**: Picture yourself floating gently on a warm, healing ocean. The water is calm and soothing, with a gentle rhythm that relaxes you deeply. Visualize the sights, sounds, and feelings of this place, and let yourself fully immerse in its calming and rejuvenating energy.
2. **Describe the Ocean**: Think about the details of the ocean. Are there gentle waves, a warm sun overhead, and the soft sounds of water lapping around you? How does it feel to be in this place of tranquility and healing?

Step 4: Visualizing a Healing Light

1. **Visualize a Healing Light**: Imagine a warm, glowing light above you. This light represents healing energy and positivity. See the light

gently descending and surrounding your entire body.

2. **Describe the Light**: Think about how this light looks and feels. Is it a soft, golden glow with a warm and comforting energy? How does it feel to be bathed in this healing light?

Step 5: Focusing on the Injury or Surgery Site

1. **Identify the Affected Area**: Bring your attention to the area of your body where you have had surgery or experienced an injury. Visualize this area clearly and focus on its sensations.
2. **Describe the Area**: Think about how this area looks and feels. Is there swelling, redness, or discomfort? How does it affect your overall sense of well-being?

Step 6: Directing the Healing Light

1. **Visualize the Light Penetrating the Area**: Imagine the healing light gently penetrating the affected area. See the light flowing into the tissue, cells, and muscles, bringing warmth and comfort.
2. **Feel the Healing**: As the light flows through the area, feel a sense of healing and rejuvenation. Imagine the light repairing damaged cells, reducing inflammation, and promoting faster healing.

Step 7: Enhancing the Healing Process

1. **Visualize the Ocean's Healing Power**: Picture the warm, healing water of the ocean gently washing over the affected area. Imagine the water carrying away any pain, discomfort, and inflammation, leaving the area refreshed and renewed. See any wounds healing completely.
2. **Feel the Progress**: As you visualize the ocean's healing power, feel the progress being made. Imagine the area becoming stronger, healthier, and more resilient with each passing moment.

Step 8: Positive Suggestions for Accelerated Healing

While floating in the healing ocean, give yourself some positive suggestions to reinforce your commitment to faster recovery. Repeat these affirmations to yourself:

1. "My body has an incredible ability to heal quickly and efficiently."
2. "Every day, I am getting stronger and healthier."
3. "I am filled with healing energy and positivity."
4. "My body is repairing itself perfectly."
5. "I am grateful for my body's ability to heal and recover."

Step 9: Embracing the Healing

1. **Visualize Embracing Your Health**: Imagine embracing your body with gratitude and appreciation. Visualize yourself fully healed, engaging in activities you love, and feeling vibrant and energetic.
2. **Feel the Empowerment**: As you embrace this new state of health, feel a sense of empowerment and confidence. Know that you are on a path of healing and positive change.

Step 10: Returning to Reality

1. **Return from the Visualization**: Imagine gradually returning from your visualization, bringing all the healing and positivity from the exercise with you. See yourself leaving the healing ocean but knowing the benefits stay with you.
2. **Re-enter the Calming Place**: Visualize coming back to your calming place, feeling even more determined and ready to support your body's healing process.

Step 11: Returning to Wakefulness

When you are ready to end the session, imagine leaving your calming place, feeling refreshed and empowered. Count up from one to five. With each count, feel yourself becoming more alert and ready to engage in your day. By the count of five, open your eyes, feeling refreshed and in control.

Chapter 21: Your Hypnotic Journey

Congratulations! You've reached the end of our journey together, but this is just the beginning for you. With the knowledge and tools you've gained, you're now equipped to tackle life's challenges and create the future you desire. Keep practicing, stay curious, and enjoy the incredible power of self-hypnosis.

Remember, self-hypnosis is a journey, not a destination. Each step you take brings you closer to mastering this powerful tool and transforming your life in ways you never imagined. Happy hypnotizing!

For more information on hypnosis, or the other modalities I use in my practice such as Neuro-linguistic Programming, Eye Movement Integration, or Resonant Frequency Therapy, visit my website at www.mindoverthebody.com[1].

For more information on becoming a board-certified hypnotherapist through my accredited training school, Hypno-Mastery, visit www.hypno-mastery.com[2]

---

1. http://www.mindoverthebody.com

2. http://www.hypno-mastery.com

Don't miss out!

Visit the website below and you can sign up to receive emails whenever Tim Moore publishes a new book. There's no charge and no obligation.

https://books2read.com/r/B-A-RGURB-TFLPD

BOOKS 2 READ

Connecting independent readers to independent writers.